WILD BORN

R.J. Young

authorHOUSE®

AuthorHouse™
1663 Liberty Drive
Bloomington, IN 47403
www.authorhouse.com
Phone: 1 (800) 839-8640

Published by AuthorHouse 07/15/2017

ISBN: 978-1-4918-4379-6 (sc)
ISBN: 978-1-4918-4378-9 (e)

Library of Congress Control Number: 2013922825

Print information available on the last page.

Any people depicted in stock imagery provided by Thinkstock are models, and such images are being used for illustrative purposes only. Certain stock imagery © Thinkstock.

This book is printed on acid-free paper.

Because of the dynamic nature of the Internet, any web addresses or links contained in this book may have changed since publication and may no longer be valid. The views expressed in this work are solely those of the author and do not necessarily reflect the views of the publisher, and the publisher hereby disclaims any responsibility for them.

Author's Note

A thank you to my lovely wife for believing that
I could and gave me the hope I needed.
And a very special thank you to my friend who
read it first and Inspired me to continue.

Chapter 1

The Wedding

I don't know what made me do it, I don't know what was possibly going through my head. But I do know as she touched my skin with a caress so soft and genuine, I knew that she was the one for me. When our lips pressed together in the softest most wonderful moment I felt as though the world fell beneath my feet. I felt as though I was falling not in the bad way that you see in movies or reading any kind of book but the way it feels when the one that you love the most is holding you close and watching as though you are their whole world, their whole galaxy.

I'm getting ahead of myself though my name is Tara LaRenge and this is my story of how I found myself. My true self the one that I always hid away from my parents my friends my family everyone who I ever held dear only know the lies that I told but it was a lie of omission not because I wanted to hurt them but because I wanted to save myself. It all started on a very hot day one of the hottest that we've had all year it hasn't rained yet but everyone knew it was coming that's what you get for living in Maine I suppose. But what I saw that day really opened my eyes to the possibility of being myself. I lived in a town of approximately 2000 people there's not much to this town I mean there's a stoplight and a little bookstore. I've visited there quite a few times it was one of my favorite spots they never really had too many new items but that wasn't the reason I would go there you see there was this girl she was 18 years old and had long dark hair the kind that could be put up in a ponytail and would look shiny and beautiful in whatever lighting she stayed in. She always had these giant nerdy glasses on but they always made her look so serious. I would oftentimes go there every time I would hear my parents fighting it was almost a constant thing in my household anymore. It got really bad when my cousin Jeremy came out of the closet he used to visit me over the summers and we would walk down to the beach play in the water a little bit he was 3 years older than me but when he came out to his parent their belief system got in the way and pushed him out as soon as he turned 18. That was always my biggest fear because not only was Jeremy my best friend but he was the only one that knew the truth about me and when I saw what had happened it had kept me in what seems like a cage. I wasn't free to do what I wanted or look the way I wanted I felt as though I was judged here every single action or gesture I used was just another lie. It felt like a fire I once had, had slowly started dying and I couldn't do anything about it. Things that set these events in motion was the wedding invitation that Jeremy had sent to my parent he was marrying the love is life and it was beautiful, a deep cream envelope with beautiful gold trim showing their names Jeremy and Thomas cordially inviting you to attend the wedding of the century. It looked as though they had spared no expense in planning their beautiful day but as I watched my parents reactions they looked as though they might be sick. They began yelling horrible slurs towards the gay community saying how "God" wouldn't want them to be the way they were, the way they were born.

The way.
I.
Was.
Born.

As I realized what the reaction meant I saw that I would never be able to be myself. They would always hold me on this pedestal that they placed me on and I would never be able to escape. That's what really set the gears in motion that's why I ran. So in the dead of night on the next day I collected all of the money I had saved working at odd jobs over the summers and hopped onto the bus it was an old beat down bus station that took me forever to walk to but I did. I bought a ticket to New York. I was 19 years old more than old enough to move out. I didn't take my phone with me just left a note taped to the fridge I knew they would see it. With just a simple words *"I love you, I know you won't feel the same way about me when I tell you this but I'm Gay."*

I didn't know exactly where Jeremy and Thomas lived but I had the envelope that they had sent their wedding invitation with. I had swiped it before my father could shred it like he did to the invitation and I figured I could always ask for directions when I got there? This seemed like a good plan at the time. When the bus pulled out of the station it was as though the cage door had opened the bird had flown the shackles had broken but I knew I was just moments away from finally being free of the religious bigotry that followed my family everywhere no matter where I went in this world I knew it could always be right around the corner.

The bus pulled out of the station it took a very long time what seems like forever to finally see the beautiful city lights of New York City I slept maybe 3-4 hours tops but I was just so excited to get there and I realize that bus ticket cost a lot more money than I thought. I would need to have a job in New York to start my life. But what can one person do in a giant city besides start a life? I've asked myself that question every day and I think I finally found my answer. As I looked at the buildings on the streets and all the people running back and forth so fast needing to get somewhere it wasn't as calm or as quiet as my little hometown but I was very excited I could feel my palms begin to sweat as the bus pulled into a station I grabbed my luggage I only had one suitcase filled with clothing that would fit me and of course a bag of toiletries and a couple little things I had brought from home the one thing that stuck out though was the last book I bought at the bookshop it was just a cheesy romantic vampire story some sort of fruit on the front of the cover if I remember correctly but these things were now everything I had in the world, as I walked up the street with my little bag I began looking around and finding myself in the city and realizing just how big it is it's one of the largest cities in the world at least that's what I thought coming from the small town anyway.

I began looking for some sort of map or guide and instead came upon an a police officer on a horse he was very kind as kind as a New Yorker can be anyway. I showed him the address and he told me to just go a couple blocks I didn't realize how close I was to my best friend in the whole world I was moments away from seeing Jeremy finally meeting his partner Thomas. I was absolutely terrified. what if he turns me away or what if he calls my parents they don't know where I'm at they don't probably even know I've left yet. I find myself standing in front of a beautiful sandstone building seeing all of the windows gleaming with sunlight and I open the giant glass door and walk up the stairs to apartment 52 B I probably could have taken the elevator but I needed some time to think of what I was going to say how would I even explain that to Jeremy. would he understand?

Looking at the past now it seemed almost laughable to have these feelings but the trepidation was real I walked up to the door took a deep breath and knocked.

Chapter 2

Arrival

A man I didn't recognize open the door he was tall with dark brown hair had a very sweet looking face and was wearing a brightly colored plaid shirt with very tight jeans I still wonder how he got into them. But he gave me a look up and down and with a kind look of concern when he saw my bag.

"Can I help you?" the man asked politely.

This was my chance my mouth and dried up as though I hadn't had water in weeks I felt my hands shaking and I showed him the envelope it had turned into a bit of a wrinkled mess on the way up the stairs but the look in his eyes deepened as he looked at the beautiful embroidered envelope and when he saw the name he looked up at me again.

"My name is Tara and I'm Jeremy's cousin I would like to speak to him if he's available please?" everything I just said came out no higher than a whisper but the man was very kind pulled me into the apartment and told me "Wait right here I'll go get him sit down if you like. You look like you might fall over." as he rushed off to go get Jeremy.

I looked at the living room area and slowly sat down on the couch. My knees began shaking, my palms drenched in sweat, my hair sticking to the nape of my neck.

NO! Pull yourself together Tara you can do this! Jeremy will understand he's been through this too.

I could hear the sound of footsteps echoing on the hardwood floor. As I look up I see Jeremy there the first thing I notice about him is that his face had changed since I'd last seen him. He looked older? And had a nice 5 o'clock shadow growing in, the next thing I noticed was that he was soaked and holding a towel around his waist.

"Tara?" he whispered my name quietly, then cleared his throat "What the hell are you doing here? Are you okay?"

The man from before slowly walked in with a confused look on his face.

"Jeremy..." I tried to speak but the words wouldn't come to me. *What the hell are you doing this is your chance! Say something. ANYTHING!* "I. Jeremy I ran away, I'm so sorry to ask this but can I stay here with you guys?" everything came out in a rush, I could feel something wet falling down my face, when I reached up to feel what it was my eyes began leaking very quickly.

"Tara what happened? Are you hurt? Oh my god. Tom what

do we do?" Jeremy rushed to my side in an instant and was hugging me to his bare chest The man who I assume was Tom sat on my other side and began rubbing my back.

"Sweetie pie what happened? Were you kicked out?" Tom asked me gingerly as he continued to rub my back. "You are more than welcome to stay with us... Here." He reached into his breast pocket and pulled out a bright hot pink handkerchief and gently placed it into my hand. "don't worry about anything just relax" I dabbed my eyes gently.

"Jeremy you gotta get to work. Don't worry sweetheart he's gonna be back later" I guess he noticed the look of panic my face had taken on "I'll put you on a pot of tea and you can tell me everything okay?"

Jeremy jumped up from the couch and raced into a room. I could see the shadow running back and forth I suppose putting on clothing, because the next instant he came out in a tweed jacket with patches on the elbows and very nice dress pants with a suitcase in hand I have to go Tara but I will be back later my class only goes till about 3 today but don't worry, I'll take care of you and we'll figure all this out okay just don't go anywhere stay with Tom he's off for the day you should be fine. Tom I want you to watch her like a hawk she's a sneaky one." He said with a smile as he raced out the door to what I assumed was his job. With a sigh Tom got up and walked to the kitchen. I looked up with a sniff and walked towards the noise of a gas stove firing up. Peeking in I saw Tom putting a black kettle on the burner the light scrape of metal resounded quietly. With a deep sigh I pulled myself off of the couch and slowly walked into the kitchen area. Looking around I noticed the very pristine concrete counter tops with a draping bar that held the sink, the teal barstools placed in a nice neat row of three with a cup sitting in front of one. A small tag was hanging out of it with a brand lable.

"What kind of tea do you normally drink? Personally I love lemon zest tea in the morning but you look like an english breakfast sort of person." Tom smiled with a kindness that was all very new to me.

"I love english breakfast it's one of my favorites." I said clearing my throat in a very unladylike manner. "This is a beautiful home you guys have here."

With a light chuckle Tom wandered over to the stove and reached up into the cabinet to pull out a small selection of tea bags, paging through them with expert fingers he chose one in a reddish brown pouch and gently opened it. Walking across the kitchen he opened another cabinet and pulled out a light gray mug with green ceramic inside it. Plopping the bag in the teapot on the stove began shrilling like a train ready to leave the station. Grabbing a dish towel Tom grasped the handle of the pot and began pouring it lightly into the cup till it was just a half inch away from the rim. With both pot and cup in hand he gently slid the cup towards me and poured more water into his own cooled cup and sat the kettle back onto the stove.

"Sugar?" Tom looked over at me with a smile and slowly slid a little white pot that had a small wooden spoon sticking out of it, the bowl itself was beautiful, with cursive lettering on the bottom declaring the contents to be sugar. The top of said bowl had deep brown lines in it as though it had sat in a panini press for some time. With delicate fingers I opened the jar and spooned in 3 scoops into my cup and replaced the spoon back into the jar. Blowing on the steaming tea in my cup I took a tiny sip, it tasted like the kind of tea I had back home. I could feel my eyes beginning to water again and dabbed them gently with the gaudy handkerchief that I had been clinging to in my hands.

"Jeremy loves this brand, he says it reminds him of home... And if I am seeing you correctly, it seems to me that you are having the same issue?" Tom took a sip of his own cup before continuing. "Stop me if I'm wrong sweetheart, but it also seems to me that you are having a bit of a problem with your family? Perhaps the same kind that Jeremy is having with them accepting him as he is?" Mutely I nodded but before I could say anything Tom had already pressed on.

"And just by looking at you, I'm guessing here again. Is that you left home in hopes of building a new life for yourself? Perhaps coming to the big city to find oh I don't know... Love? A home? Am I reading you correctly so far?" Tom smiled sweetly.

"Yes..." My voice felt as though it was going to give out when a knock on the door interrupted my thought process.

Chapter 3

Community

Looking towards the family room Tom stood up and walked to the door. I could hear a quiet conversation between Tom and one other person.

"Tara? Can you please come here? I have someone I want you to meet." Tom's voice sounded cheerful given the sudden appearance of someone.

Getting up from my stool I walked into the living area and peeked around the corner. Looking past Tom's form in the doorway I noticed a lovely young woman in her early 20's wearing a green apron. Her hair fell past her shoulders in deep chocolate waves, she had dark skinny jeans on with what looked like stains of paint. In fact her cheek had a light blue smear on it and there was yellow and purple streaks in her hair. Her arms had light green speckles all over them with deep purple along her breasts. The brushes that she held in her apron pocket looked worn but well loved and used.

"Tara? This is Zoey Lewis, she's one of our neighbors. Zoey this is Jeremy's cousin, she…. well let's just say she let the cat out of the bag" Tom said lightly with a chuckle.

The girl named Zoey looked over at me with a gentle smile. "Hi Tara, it's a pleasure to meet you. Tom focus. FOCUS. I need those design plans if we are ever going to get anywhere with the Hampton decor. I can't just willy-nilly throw paint on the wall and hope it sticks. The plans you sent me look like something out of a bad 80's film"

Puffing his cheeks out Tom looked over at me "Sorry Tara I need to hold off on our conversation for a bit." Looking over at Zoey quickly "You. You may come in but try to stay in the kitchen area, it took me over a week to get the paint off the hardwood last time and I would appreciate it if you would put a towel down or something next time."

"Oh Bitch Bitch Bitch. Shouldn't you be offering me tea and crumpets or are you just gonna be a drama queen all day. Don't worry I'll stay in the kitchen." Glancing over at me she gave a playful wink. "And maybe Tara, can keep me company?"

"I do not bitch you bitch." Tom said puffing up like a balloon. "Ignore here Tara she thinks she's the hottest lesbian in the building or something."

"I think she's pretty hot." The words left my mouth before I could stop them and from the very pregnant pause that followed Tom was shocked that I had responded in such a manner. What sounded like a snort came from Zoey who started giggling loudly. "SEE Tom I'm Pretty Hot. Come on Tara, you can tell me what other parts you think are hot." Zoey said to me in a way that butterflies filled my stomach and made my heart pound like a drum. I watched her walk into the kitchen area with a light swing of her hips, the feeling that burst through my heart as though I could feel her siren call. Following after her like a lost puppy I wandered into the kitchen and noticed she had grabbed what looked to be a ratty old towel and had draped it over one of the stools. She was reaching up into the cabinet and was just a few inches too short to grab the nearest coffee cup. Walking up behind her I reached over her hand and grabbed the handle for her and gently lowered it down to her.

Her skin was like fire as she slowly turned to face me, her eyes looking directly into mine. our hips touching lightly as she brushed against me. I noticed she had glasses on the top of her head that had been covered in the same blue paint on her cheeks. Looking deep into her eyes the color of storm clouds over the ocean. Before I knew it our lips touched in a light kiss, pulling away quickly "I'm sorry. I didn't mean to do that." I looked down at my feet. The pressure of her hands cupping my face brought my eyes back up to meet hers.

"I did." Zoey took my lips captive once more and pushed me back till I was flush with the bar, I could feel the heat of our passion curling in my gut as her hands traced up and down my sides. Her hands gently searching my back and unclasped my bra through my shirt, our breathing matching wonderfully as her tongue traced my cheek

13

and down my neck. Gasping lightly she sucked on my neck till I moaned with pleasure. As quickly as it had started she was gone, Zoey's back was too me as she began fixing herself some tea, looking behind myself I could hear Tom's footsteps walking back towards us. Sitting myself back on my original stool I began fixing my hair. reaching behind me I redid my bra and began sipping my tea once more.

"Oh yes just help yourself to my tea, Next you will be asking me for food, shelter, and wa-" Zoey began pouring hot water into her cup with a little private smile.

"Was the word you were looking for Water Tom?" She said with a giggle.

"Bitch." Tom reached into his pocket to pull out his cell phone and began typing furiously. "There. I sent you the plans for the Hampton decor now shoo." he began moving his hands in a get out manner.

"Oh poo, and here I thought that you would be a good host and show me your design ideas for what you wanted to do to my apartment since and I quote." pulling out her cell phone Zoey began reading "it looks like a gay train crashed through here and brought a horde of glitter and paint with it" Looking up at him she smiled in a very teasing way successfully shutting him up. Sipping her tea she sat down on the stool with the towel and paged through the designs for the Hampton. "These are actually really great Tom. Though you forgot one thing."

"What, what are you gonna nit pick at now?" Tom said curtly.

"What color are the walls gonna be?" Zoey smiled lightly turning her phone to show a beautiful design but with only white on the walls, giving it an almost sterile look.

"I think it should be a forest green with white ceilings. It would bring just enough color to counteract the white" Again I shocked myself when I opened my mouth. "Or maybe a powder blue? it would help to make the room look bigger without being just all white... or something"

Zoey studied the picture for a small time longer before responding. "I think you're right on the powder blue, though maybe more of a lighter shade just to give it a bit of a sky color since the window is going right there..." Hopping down from the stool she grabbed her phone and looked at me. "I'll see what I can do about that. Also" Grabbing my face between her hands she pressed her lips firmly to mine. "Thats for the road." With a smile she wandered to the door and shut it firmly behind her.

Tom looked at me with a dumbstruck expression. "Well it looks like my little Tara is growing up." tilting his head to the side he grabbed a napkin and blotted my cheek revealing a smear of light blue. "You'll want to be careful around those lesbians they leave all sorts of things behind." He said with a chuckle.

"Is she always that affectionate? Not that I mind! But it would have been nice to have had some warning." I said sheepishly.

"Honestly no I haven't seen her this excited to meet someone since her last girlfriend. I think It's been almost 4 years since she's even shown any interest in anyone. You lucky dog. come on it's time to get some lunch in you, and some lunch in me too." Tom gently helped me off the stool and went to grab his jacket from the hall. Dutifully I followed him as he went through the closet looking for the perfect one to match his bright blue shirt. "I don't know what to wear today. Everything I've tried on so far just does not look right with this blue. Any suggestions oh great and powerful color finder?" He sighed looking at me helplessly.

"How about the charcoal gray one? it would bring out the highlights in your hair, and it would compliment the blue as well?" Grabbing the gray jacket from the hanger and holding it up to make my point.

"Hey! And here I thought lesbians didn't know a thing about fashion." Tom said with a cheeky grin as he grabbed the coat from me.

"I thought gay guys were suppose to be good with colors?" I fired back sarcastically.

A look of shock flitted across Tom's face after that sentence came out of my mouth. "Oh sweetheart that was very good but you don't want to mess with me. I'm a bear. Woof."

Chapter 4

Autumn

It had been about 3 weeks since I had fled from my imprisonment in Maine. The days passed fairly quickly and living with Jeremy and Tom was a cinch. I helped with chores around the house and had found myself a part time job at the college library making roughly 11 an hour. The work was everything I had wanted and they never had me doing too much giving me ample time to read my favorites, and some new discoveries i hadn't known about before. The ladies in the cafeteria were always sweet and let me have as much coffee as I desired throughout the day at no charge. Walking back to the sandstone building I looked up at the highrises and smiled at the amazing colors the sun played off the windows. Focusing once again I noticed 2 people standing at the entrance of my new home. The woman had hair past her hips with a long skirt that was well past her knees. The man was wearing an expression of one who has eaten something foul. They were having what seemed to be an argument about how to get into the building. As I approached closer I heard my name and stopped dead.

"Andy we have to talk some sense into her. If we don't her eternal soul will be damned to hell!"

"Stephanie I know! Are you sure this is the right building? I mean this doesn't look any different than the other ones. How do we know where the fags live?"

Looking around wildly I grab my little flip phone that Jeremy had given me and snap a picture of the two and send it to him with a text.

My parents are here I got off work early and I don't know what to do!!

Frantically I rushed between the buildings and ducked behind the dumpster there. I was still able to hear snatches of their conversation from my hiding place.

"Andy she's gonna be coming of age soon! If we don't find her by the time the full moon rises on her birthday it could be disastrous! She's the first female of your family in what 80 years?!"

"I KNOW STEPH! That's why we have to play nice with these faggots!" my father's voice kept rising higher and higher. Just like when we were at home. I had heard enough of his bitching and checked my phone for any signs that Jeremy had gotten my message. With a frantic look around I darted from my hiding spot and walked briskly out of the alleyway and in the opposite direction of my home.

Thinking for a moment of where i could go my phone buzzed with a new message. Glancing at the screen Jeremy had responded.

Go to Tom's work and wait with him, I'll be there as soon as I finish my lecture. Don't worry we won't let them near you if you don't want them there.

With a smile I began walking to the address Jeremy had made me memorize my first week living with them. It took a total of 35 minutes to get there on foot but as soon as I stepped into the lobby of Harper, Colden and Son's I felt my heart rate drop back down to normal. The receptionist looked up and forced a light smile.

"Welcome to Harper, Colden and Son's do you have an appointment?"

"Oh um no ma'am I was told to come here and see Tom?"

"Alright. Mr. Colden is currently in a meeting if you will just take a seat I will let him know that you are here. What did you say your name was again dear?" at that moment her phone rang and I could hear Tom's voice coming from the end of the receiver.

"Madeline I am waiting on someone to get here, she should arrive soon. Her name is Tara and as soon as she get here send her in. She should be wearing a hoodie with New York University's logo on it. Send her up as quickly as possible!"

The receptionist glanced my way and noticed my royal purple hoodie with the NYU logo on it and her eyes widened slightly. "Right away Mr. Colden! She just walked in." hanging up the receiver Madeline looked at me and said "Mr. Thomas is waiting for you just go down the hall and take a right the black elevator will be there and just press 315* it will open right up into his lobby. I'm sorry to have kept you waiting Ms. Tara"

Blinking quickly I felt my face heat up with embarrassment from being addressed in such a way. I muttered my thanks and began to quickly walk through the lobby and down the hallway till I reached a tall black set of elevator doors with a keypad on them. Pressing in the code the doors shot open revealing a white marbled interior. Stepping in lightly I pressed the button that had lit up. As the doors closed I looked around the small elevator box and noticed the walls were not walls at all but glass windows. As the elevator made its ascent towards Tom's office I saw the evening light spill in through the walls of the elevator and reveal a beautiful scene of New York's skyline all along the coast. The elevator buzzed lightly and the doors opened revealing a pristine marble and granite lobby with a receptionist desk. Giant walnut doors across said lobby opened up to reveal Tom looking a bit harassed.

"Tara! I'm so happy you are ok!" running over to me he swept me into a giant bear hug. "Don't worry sweetheart let's get you some tea. KELSEY!"

A twiggy redhead peeked her head from around the corner of a hallway. "Yes Tom?"

"Get my favorite cousin some English breakfast tea with 4 sugar cubes and cream on the side please. We will be in my office discussing things so just bring it in. Also reschedule my meetings for today. Something has come up and I need to deal with them, have my calls forwarded to my voicemail and have all my other meetings put into next week please."

"Right away Tom." swinging back around the corner I heard the distinct noise of water filling up a metal pan.

Gently hugging me by my shoulder Tom guided me into his office and halfway shut the door. The room was expansive and the view of New York was lovely. He guided me lightly into a giant comfy chair where I sank down gratefully. His office had a small desk in the corner of it and it looked as though it had been rarely touched. The other furniture was that of a living room rather than that of a place of business. Sitting across from me in a wing back chair he looked into my eyes.

"I got a call from Jeremy saying you saw your parents? What happened?"

Taking a deep breath I looked at Tom and told him everything I had heard. About halfway through Kelsey wandered in with a tea tray and a cup of cream on the side and closed the door behind her. I had went silent during that interruption till she had left where I continued. "I think they want to forcefully take me back."

"Sweetheart you know that we would never let them do that to you" he looked at me and grabbed my hands lightly "you are an adult and are out on your own. But you're not alone at all! Do you know what they meant by coming of age on your birthday?"

R.J. Young

"I honestly have no idea. Growing up I knew that I was the only girl in my father's side of the family but I never knew what that really meant. Do you think they were planning on doing something to me?" I could feel my voice quaver at the end of the question. It was as though a giant weight had settled in the pit of my stomach.

"Well I have never really met your family so I can't really say sugar." Tom said lightly sipping his tea. "What I do know though is if they try anything Jeremy and I are going to be right by your side stopping anything from happening to you. Okay? So don't worry your pretty little head." he said with a smile.

Glancing outside I noticed the sun had begun setting and the clouds started rolling in quickly.

"Looks like it's time to go. Just in time too, the weatherman said its suppose to be a shit storm. Thats autumn for ya I guess." with a sigh he got out of the chair and stretched lightly. "Come on let's go home. I know Jeremy should be finished with his lecture soon. Here take this." walking to the closet next to the desk Tom opened it up and grabbed a black trench coat and tossed it to me. I quickly wrapped myself in it and inhaled deeply. The scent was absolutely amazing it filled my nostrils up with the smell of fresh cut grass and fresh clay.

"Whose jacket is this?" I asked. I could have sworn I had smelled this scent before.

"It's Zoey's" Tom said with a light chuckle. "Let's go." wandering to the door he grabbed his own jacket off the back of the chair he had vacated and held the door open for me.

Chapter 5

Past

The wind was really picking up speed outside, it had been building up since that day I had seen my parents. Looking out the window of Jeremy and Tom's apartment my mind had been wandering since they had left for work. I was off today and was determined to take it easy. I just kept thinking about the questions Tom had kept asking Jeremy and myself about our home life.

"So what was it like growing up?" Tom looked at me with eyes that seemed to know too much. Jeremy shifted uncomfortably in his chair. He was sitting as far away as possible on the couch from Tom while still touching his bare feet to Tom's leg.

"It was... It was as tough I had been trapped. I wasn't able to do anything alone. Every sunday morning I was woken up by my father yelling at my mother usually between 7-8 in the morning that we were gonna be late for church.

That's what they called it anyway" with a sigh I felt the memories slowly returning. "I was forced to wear dresses or denim skirts my whole life. I was never allowed to wear pants, I couldn't cut my hair or even join in sports activities at school. Anything that they said was for men or boys I could not participate in." Tom's eyes widened slightly at this information.

"You couldn't cut your hair? Or wear pants?"

"Yeah. Every single move I made was watched like a hawk, I wanted to die. I wanted to scream at them to leave me alone." swallowing hard I could feel the tears creeping up the back of my throat and itching it lightly. "The day that Jeremy came out… I don't blame you Jeremy please believe that. But the day you had come out was the day they had watched me even more. As if you being gay was somehow contiguous, a disease I could catch." Jeremy looked down and avoided eye contact for a minute before meeting my pleading gaze.

"I considered taking my own life quite a few times. Any place I went I was stalked like a deer being hunted. I couldn't have friends over unless they were in the church. The only exception was that I had to try to convert my school friends into 'seeing the light'… It hurt to try to explain the situation I was in with my friends. I lost many of them when I tried." looking down at my hands my knuckles had gone white from the strain of holding back tears.

"When I turned 13 is when the real issues began. I had started my period and my father was none too happy about it. He would call me all sorts of things but the one thing that scarred my psyche the most was when I turned 17. I had just got off of a third shift. He had told me to clean the dishes and pick up my room. I had worked that night from 3pm-10am it was an insane shift but I had to do it. I walked into my room and looked around. Every one of my possessions were thrown all over the floor. my computer was gone my connection with the outside world was gone. I hadn't been able to clean my room because I had to take a nap so I wouldn't fall asleep at work. He took it as defiance to his order. He came up behind me and began hitting me very hard with a wooden spoon till it busted on my hands that were trying to cover and protect my head. My mother just stood in the doorway and just watched. She didn't lift a finger to help me one bit…" my voice trailed off as Tom rushes over and pulled me into a massive hug. He began to lightly pet my hair and whispered sweet things into the top of my head. Jeremy crossed the short space and hugged me from the other side as I began to weep openly for the first time in almost a month.

When we had arrived back at the sandstone fortress my parents had vanished from the stoop.

❧❧

Shaking my head lightly I sipped my tea once again and sighed. *What good is it to dwell on the past?*

Looking around the living room I noticed the black trench coat hanging on the wall hook. *I really should return that to Zoey.* Stretching lightly I relaxed further into the comfy window seat and continued to sip my tea.

Chapter 6

Real Fear

The sudden knock on the door jolted me from my thoughts. Looking around I got up and set my tea mug on the kitchen counter. Wandering over to the door I opened it a crack and was greeted with the door slamming into my face hard enough to make me see stars and knock me flat on my ass. Blinking wildly my eyes had teared up from pain and I felt something warm dripping from my nose. Looking up to the attacker I gasped as a cold pinprick stabbed my neck. The world started spinning madly then

Everything.
Went.
Dark.

Zoey

I heard a crash from upstairs with a very loud yell. It made me jump and smear orange paint all along the treeline I had finished an hour ago.

"MOTHER FUCKER!" my voice echoed all around my studio apartment. Glaring up at the ceiling I grabbed a rag and began blotting the insulting color off of the canvas. Loud footsteps could be heard from the stairwell as though someone was carrying something very heavy. With a growl I walked to the door to give whoever it was a piece of my mind for making such a racket. Grabbing the knob and swinging open the door I noticed 3 things. The first was there were three men in the hallway two of which were carrying a small brunette girl down the stairs. The second thing was the third man had a very large gun strapped to his back and was taking latex gloves off if his hands. And the third thing the girl the first two men had between them was none other than.

"TARA!" I rushed at the man with the gun first. I could feel myself shaking in fear and the sudden kick of adrenaline sent my brain into overdrive. I grabbed him by the strap of the gun and twisted so he tumbled down the stairs hitting the two men carrying Tara and causing them to all fall at once. Rushing after them I grabbed Tara from the pile of bodies and fireman carried her back up to my apartment where I locked the door.

Rushing her to the couch I looked over at the door scanned the room for a dining chair to prop under the handle.

Looking back down at her after I had successfully barred the door closed I checked for her pulse. It was weak but there, pulling out my phone I dialed Jeremy's number. The intro to his voicemail was annoyingly chipper and as soon as the beep sounded I spoke in a rush.

"Jeremy! Someone broke into your place and I think they drugged Tara. I have her with me we are safe, call me when you get this."

Tossing the phone aside I grabbed a rag and began mopping up her face. Blood had spilled out of her nose and the aroma was just so sweet...

<u>Tara</u>

My face hurt my body ached and I felt like I had drank my way through 40 shots. What did I do last night to have such a hangover? I felt a very light pressure on my face. It was cold and wet and felt amazing on my burning skin.

I felt a slight tickling sensation on my neck that made me sigh. A sudden pinching made my eyes shoot open and look down. Zoey was holding my shoulders lightly and her face was burried in my neck. With a gasp I felt a burning sensation that made me cry out in pain. Zoey's head shot up to look at me. Her stormy gray eyes had changed to a deep purple and had slits like a cat, the lips that had kissed me so tenderly were drawn back in an aggressive manner with blood smeared all along her cheek. The one thing that had caught my eye most was her canine teeth had elongated to dagger like pinpricks and were curved inwardly like a snake. Her hands tightened their grip on my shoulders almost painfully.

That was the last thing I remember before I passed out cold again.

I woke up in a cool dark room on a bed that felt like clouds. I could hear soft music playing beyond the closed door, it was orchestral music that swelled and danced till the notes faded to silence once again. Looking around I noticed I was in my underwear and bra, and I could hear footsteps pattering around the other room. A new symphony started up and the music swelled again. The sheets I had been laid upon were soft and smelled like honeysuckle and rain. The images of the strange dream came swooping back up at me from the dark. Pointed teeth, the beautiful and dangerous face of Zoey, blood everywhere. My heart began pounding, when I turned my head to sit up I felt a soft tugging on my skin. Reaching my hand up I felt a soft cottony bandage that had been taped there. Looking around I noticed an aluminum baseball bat propped up in the corner, the shine had caught my eye from the crack beneath the door. Slowly I sat up and placed my feet to the floor, taking a few easy steps I shuffled my way to the bat. I felt like I had gotten a bout of the flu that my body had been trying to fight off. Grasping the bat firmly in hand I slowly made my way to the door. Gripping the door handle I heard a voice coming from the other side.

"I KNOW JEREMY! I said I was sorry! She was just-.... Yes I know she's your cousin but how else was I to stop the bleeding!?... I think they knocked her face in with something..... Yes. Of course. She's resting now. Yes I'm sure she had a pulse. I checked it before and after I bit her."

After she what me?! My mind was racing at this new

information I pressed my ear closer to the door in hopes of hearing better.

"She is fine. She was delirious. I'm pretty sure she won't remember a damn thing about it. I did taste something that wasn't suppose to be there. She had quite a bit of Rohypnol in her system. From the looks of it they put it right in her neck. I was able to drain most of it out before it circulated her system too much….. Don't worry I'll have her stay with me till you get home. I threw her in my bed and tossed her clothing in the wash to get the blood off so she kinda has to stay for a bit till they dry."

Well that explains where my clothing went… What is Rohypnol?

"Yeah she's gonna be okay- …. No the police came here and the attackers had already left. I didn't get a good look at them but one had quite a large gun. Yes…. Okay Jeremy I'll text you when she wakes up. Bye" Zoey's voice ceased and the music turned up to a higher volume. Taking a deep breath I slowly inched the door open.

Peeking down the hall I saw her standing with her back to me painting what looked to be a beautiful forest landscape, a streak of orange had marred the far right side of the canvas. Getting a firmer grip on the bat I slowly stepped into the hall. My heart was pounding a mile a minute, my breath started to catch lightly. I could feel the adrenaline rush starting. Creeping slowly towards Zoey I noticed she was wearing a tight fitting pair of shorts and a white cami top with her green apron I had first seen her in. I took a few more steps till i was almost three feet behind her. My foot found the one creaky spot on the floor. Her back stiffened with her paintbrush poised inches above the canvas. Slowly she lowered the brush and turned her head till I could see the corner of her left eye. Her lips were pursed and her jaw began working as though she was swallowing a very large pill.

"Tara? Are-... What are you doing out of bed?" her voice was falsely light and singsong.

I had raised the bat like a pro hitter and planted my feet.

"I want answers. Put the brush down and turn towards me slowly or I bash your head in."

Slowly she lowered the paintbrush into her green apron and brought both hands to shoulder height. Carefully she turned towards me. Her eyes never leaving my own.

"Good." lowering my bat carefully my voice faltered a little bit at the fear and determination in her eyes. "I..." my voice was caught in my throat. Her face looked as though she had witnessed someone die, causing my resolve to waiver. "Zoey... thank you. For saving me from those people." a spark of relief crossed her face showing the barest hint of a smile her front teeth peeked out from her upper lip reminding me of the images. Noticing my face a look of concern crossed her own.

"Tara sweetie why don't we sit down to talk? You still look exhausted" gently lowering her hands she edged away from me towards the couch where she sat as graceful as a swan.

The only thing that gave away her uneasiness was her fingers drumming on her leg lightly.

Still holding the bat firmly I walked to the opposite end of the couch and sat down. My eyes never leaving her face.

"Did you... did you clean me up?" I asked, unsure of how to broach the subject.

"Of course. I couldn't let you bleed out all over the hallway. So I brought you in here laid you in the bed and bandaged you up. Your clothing is in the washing machine. It looks like your nose took a beating." as she said all this she wouldn't look me in the eyes. I could almost see the wheels turning in her head trying to get out of talking with me. "I didn't want you to wake up in a panic so I played some soft music to help you relax. I think they drugged you up. You were saying all sorts of strange things."

The little voice in the back of my head was screaming at me *SHE'S LYING TO YOU CAN'T YOU SEE THAT!? SHE WON'T EVEN LOOK AT YOU!* Taking a deep breath I set the bat on the floor.

"Thank you for doing all of that. It was very kind of you. But I want to know... what are you not telling me Zoey?"

Her eyes slowly met mine and I could see a resolve forming behind the beautiful stormy gray, her jaw began tensing and without warning, all the color drained from her face causing her skin to go the color of printer paper. Her mouth opened slightly "I-" the washing machine alarm buzzed through the empty apartment causing both of us to jump. "I better go get that so they can dry off." rising up from her seat she rushed past the small kitchen into a small laundry room where sounds of a washer opening and clothes being thrown into a dryer were heard.

Getting up from my own chair I wandered towards the noises and peeked in. She was bent over picking up a laundry basket that was brimming with paint stained clothing. Gathering up my own nerve, I walked up behind her into a hug causing her to yelp in fear. Her body tensed as I hugged, laying my head on her shoulder blade I slowly kissed her neck. A light shiver ran down her spine. She dropped the basket of clothes and slowly turned till we were facing each other. Her hands found me and her fingers traced up my arms leaving goosebumps in their wake. Looking into her eyes I slowly leaned in. Her lips captured my own and her body connected with mine. Her fingers lept into my hair tangling into the curled mess. Our breathing became ragged with passion for eachothers touch.

"Bedroom?" I said around her lips. With a grunt she lifted me into the air so I was clinging with my legs around her as she darted us to the bedroom.

Slamming the door behind us she threw me onto the bed and was atop me before I had stopped bouncing. I grabbed her cami top and began tugging upwards. Her milky breasts fell out from the shirt as she wiggled it off. Reaching for her I brought my face to her nipple. Both of them were pierced and had started engorging as I flicked my tongue back and forth over them. As she started moving her hips I flipped us so she was on her back and I laying on her. Biting lightly at the rings she moaned deeply till her hands found my hair again.

"Please go harder. Bite me harder." Zoey begged as she pressed my head closer to her skin.

I obliged to her pleas and bit down till I felt the metal scraping my teeth. Her nails dug into my scalp as she cried out in pleasure. Looking up at her I saw a light bead of sweat forming on her brow. Slowly rising up I captured her lips with mine once again and kissed her softly, her teeth took my bottom lip hostage as she sucked lightly and the little jolts of pain rocketed through me.

My hands traced down her body until the left found her other nipple while my right kept moving further south. I teased the button of her shorts and caressed the exposed skin of her stomach. Slowly I slipped two fingers into the waistband of her shorts. I felt a pop as her hands had moved down my back to my bra, she had undone the clasps there and was slipping it down my shoulders. With a frown I sat up and removed it. Her hands traced down her own body and undid her own shorts. Slipping her thumbs into the waistline she slid everything down her legs till they were on the floor.

My eyes hungrily swept down her body taking in her pale skin and perky breasts, a spot on her stomach caught my eye. The skin was puckered and looked as though she had been stabbed. It was no bigger than a quarter but my thumb rubbed absentmindedly over the blemish.

"What's wrong?" her voice wavered. "Are-... Are you okay?" her eyes trailed down to where my thumb had been rubbing. Sorrow filled her face making her eyes puff up with unshed tears. Zoey sat up quickly pulling her legs under her. She grabbed her clothes from the floor and threw them on her body.

"Wait what's wrong?!" I asked with shock "did-"

"Its nothing." I could hear the venom dripping from her every word "I shouldn't even have let you do what you did. Just- just get out." it felt as though the temperature of the room went icy.

"No. Not till I get answers" I sat up straight and glared at her. "What did I do to make you shut down? Did I hurt you? Is it because we aren't the same species? Can you not... can you not get e-excited by a human?" I felt like I had developed a cotton farm in my mouth.

"No!" Zoey grabbed my hands tightly till her knuckles turned white. "Never say that don't ever think that! I just... the last time I had been with another... being, she-..." her voice hitched. "She found out that I was, d-different and during our intimate moment she grabbed a knife out of her pocket and... she-... she stabbed me" Zoey lifted her shirt up to reveal the scar once more. She must have seen the look of fear and shock on my face because she spoke very fast. "It didn't hurt I swear! Just a little pinch... but I never went around her when I was hungry she walked in here one day while I was feeding. I had brought this woman up so I wouldn't be tempted to bite her. While I was feeding from her neck Patrice walked in and accused me of cheating. I looked at her and my fangs were still out, the escort had fainted... we talked for hours after she calmed down and she went home. I was convinced that she wouldn't want to see me again. I was shocked when she called and asked to come over." Zoey's voice had turned husky. "She came an hour later and we went to the bedroom and well... yeah" looking up her eyes pleaded with my own for understanding.

"I- I'm confused" I said tilting my head with a small smile. "Why do you want me to go?"

Zoey's mouth dropped open in shock. "You- you don't want to leave? Now that you... know that you know what I am?"

"Of course not." I said leaning in "I'm falling for you Zoey Lewis." I silenced any other protests she may have had with a kiss. We then resumed what we had started.

Her hands were like ice on my burning skin, pressing close to me she had flipped our position so that she was sitting on my stomach and had crouched over me like a graceful hunting cat, her body arched into me as she let out a wild snarl. Her tongue snaked out and licked my neck while her hand gently peeled the bandage off of me. Her lips found my pulse point and began sucking lightly. I could feel her quiver with anticipation as her teeth grazed my skin.

"Bite me." the words stopped her dead, she stiffened like a dog on point. Her head began to raise from me. Before she could move however I grabbed her by the nape and forced

her head back into my neck. "It's ok. Just do it. I want to...
I want to know."

Looking down at her elegant form I noticed her skin had
gone pasty white again. Her hands gripped my shoulders
and without warning a twinge of pain shot through my
spine though shortly a gentle pulling sensation stopped me
from struggling, as it continue pleasure bloomed in my belly.
My free hand traced down her front and dipped to her shorts
where it worked to unclasp them. Working the zipper down
Zoey moaned in anticipation.

My finger trailed along her underwear till I found the folds
between her legs, the fabric was soaked from excitement.
Gently I moved the crotch of the underwear to the side and
began stroking her most private place. Gasping in ecstasy
her fangs slid from my throat. The sensation was nothing
I had ever experienced before. I began stroking the inner
folds with two fingers, running them between each twist.
My thumb searched eagerly for her clitoris, weaving in and
out of the light dusting of hair she had down there. Her head
jerked back suddenly when I found it.

Her hand shot between us and held my hand to stop the
motion. "Do you want me to lose my head?" she hissed
playfully. Her eyes had begun glowing the deep purple of
my dreams she smiled a secretive smile as her fangs poked
out slightly over her bottom lip. "It's my turn to pleasure
you" releasing my hand she slid down my body.

Frowning slightly I asked "what are you doing?" she had
taken my underwear past my knees and was slowly dipping

her head into my crotch. "Why are yo-" my voice slipped from my throat and came out in a moan. I had never experienced anything like this feeling before. Her tongue had shot out of her mouth and was snaking its way between each layer of skin flicking up and down lightly when reaching the peak. Time had no meaning anymore. I wasn't sure how long she had stayed between my legs. I just knew I never wanted her to stop. With a final flutter of her tongue, a great crashing sensation rolled over my body. I screamed in pleasure and once it had subsided I blacked out. Right before the darkness consumed me my mind threw out a thought.

This is the best first time ever...

Zoey

This is the best first time ever...

As Tara passed out I heard her say those words that dropped ice into my stomach my heart began racing. *Her first time?! This was her first FUCKING time!? WHAT THE ACTUAL FUCK! ... Shit Jeremy is gonna slaughter me! I took is favorite cousins virginity! Shit! How could she not tell me this!*

Getting up from between her legs I noticed the blood pooling on the sheets. I reached over and grabbed a handful of tissues off the bedside table and began dabbing at the red. My mouth had drawn into a hard line as I mopped up the mess.

After it had been cleaned well enough to not startle her I wandered into the living room to grab myself something to drink. I was just so thirsty! I hadn't had any blood since yesterday except for the little tablespoon amount I had been given from Tara. I peeked into the mini fridge I had hidden under my sink and pulled out the blood bag. *I shouldn't have bit her I could have taken too much...*

Looking at the bag I could feel the hunger burning into my gut. My fangs elongated till they were dangerous points. I could suddenly hear every living person in the building their heartbeats pounding in my ears. With a strike like a cobra I felt my fangs sink in through the plastic, I moaned in ecstasy as the blood hit my system. With a shiver my mind thought back to what Tara had been doing with my nipples. I felt my skin tighten in anticipation.

The bag drained before I was full and I quickly grabbed another one. *I had to get rid of this hunger before I went back to her. If I were to not stop myself...* I shivered at the thought.

Looking around my kitchen I bit the bag once more and examined the glass cabinets for some sort of plastic cup to fill with more blood. Frowning I noticed an old drive through styrofoam cup in the garbage. Grabbing it quickly I opened the mini fridge again and grabbed another bag. Pouring it in the cup I sealed the lid on again as I finished my current bag.

Mental note. Get plastic cups with lids in case she stays over at night. Wandering out of the kitchen I grabbed a book off the side table and went back into the bedroom. Closing the door behind myself I felt my eyes shift into hunting mode. Tara's form was completely exposed, she had flipped onto her stomach her legs were spread eagle and her most beautiful spot was waiting to be used once again.

Shaking my head at her I grabbed the blanket and tossed it over her lightly so she wouldn't catch a chill from me. Climbing into the bed I propped myself up on the headboard and began reading.

Chapter 7

Pleasure or Pain

Tara

I woke to darkness I could just make out the form of Zoey sitting propped up on the headboard. Her knees were bent up and her eyes glowed eerily in the dark. With a yawn I stretched my arms out to stroke her leg lightly.

"Hey" my voice cracked a bit. My mouth was oddly dry.

"Hey yourself. Would you like a light on so you can see?" her voice sounded false and she had yet to look at me.

"No not really… Zoey whats wrong?"

"Oh nothing's wrong per say… just why didn't you tell me?"

"Tell you what?

"That this was your first time." her voice had hardened as her eyes looked into me it felt like I was being x-rayed.

Silence stretched for a moment as I thought about my answer. "How did you-"

"You said it outloud when you orgasmed. I don't mind it's just I would have made it better for you. Rather than rushing you into something that you might regret later." her eyes drooped slightly as her voice turned sad.

"Regret?" with a snorting laugh "I enjoyed the hell out of this! The whole experience! Did you... did you enjoy yourself?"

"Of course I did but you kinda passed out before we finished" reaching over me she clicked a light on the bedside table. Her nipple was right within mouths reach.

"Oh! Well then let me make it up to you" I said playfully. Gripping her torso I pulled her chest down till I had her nipple in my mouth. I began sucking with vigor till her body loosened up enough to hug her close.

"I wanna try doing what you did for me... down here." I said around her breast as my hand slid slowly down her body till it found the crease between her legs again. The folds between her legs had become slick just after a few slow caresses to them. Dipping my fingers into the juices I brought my fingers to my lips.

Her eyes widened as she watched me lick the wetness off. Biting her lip her fangs began elongating till they were pinpricks once again. Grabbing her by the hips I moved her gently till her rear was facing skyward over my face. Her breath caught when I dipped my tongue into her honey pot. I felt the blanket that had been covering my legs get thrown unceremoniously to the floor. Her face pressed close to my thigh.

"C-can I…" Her voice shook as I licked again.

"Bite me Zoey. This is all about you now." with a low growl I felt pain shoot up my leg from where she had gotten me. Her hands searched down my body till she found my own sweet spot. I had become wet with excitement myself as she flicked and rubbed my privates. Digging my tongue deeper into her I tried to match the pace of her fingers. Her toes had begun curling as I went faster the pain on my leg had subsided to a low throbbing as her fingers teased the sweetness between my legs.

With a loud yell of an explanative we both orgasmed. Her body shook for a moment as my heartrate slowly returned to normal.

I felt her fangs slowly slide from my skin and a warm wet stroke over the punctures told me she had cleaned my leg off. With a sated sigh she gently swung her leg over my head and crawled up my body to lay next to me. Looking down into her eyes I saw her pupils return to the normal rounded shape as the amethyst color faded back to her stormy gray. With a smile she leaned up and kissed me gently.

"Absolutely wonderful." she said in an almost purr. "I would love to show you the ropes a bit more maybe a bit later?" her hand trailed down my body till she was stroking the pubic hair and teasing the edge of my clit.

"What do you have in mind?" I asked in a moan as my body arched involuntarily.

"Well" she said tugging the hairs gently. "Perhaps we can try something with a toy?" she purred in my ear again. "I mean we are both naked. And you are very, very wet right now" she said as she Dipped the tips of her fingers into me.

With a shiver I nodded vigorously "show me" I moaned pleading.

Zoey

Her skin was fire on my cold hands. I dipped my fingers into her sweet wetness till my hand was soaked. A ball of passion was building between us once again. Slipping my fingers out I reached over to my bedside table and dug in the drawers till I found a fairly long dildo. It was midnight blue and had a curved end on it that was meant to be inserted into one person while the other end was penis shaped.

Showing her the toy her eyes widened a bit then lit up with excitement. The look of wanting on her face sealed the deal for me.

"Here" I held the tip that would be inserted into myself to her lips. "I need you to make this as wet as possible." I said grinning widely.

Her mouth opened slightly before she took the whole end into it and began sucking. She moaned with excitement and the sound rocketed through my spine as she did so.

After a few seconds I tugged it lightly and it pulled out of her mouth with a pop. Sitting up I opened my legs and gently pressed the end into myself till I was flush with the base. Biting my lip lightly I shivered with excitement I could feel my cheeks reddening with light embarrassment. My eyes had begun changing again as she watched me. Getting up to my knees I looked at her.

"Now my dear. I need you to suck till you feel it is ready to enter you." her eyes met mine and a flash of fear crawled through them. Getting up on her hands and knees she took the penis tip in her mouth and began sucking till it had become wet and dripped with saliva.

"Lay back and just relax." I said with a grin as she finished.

Her eyes widened more as I crawled gently on top of her. I leaned down and whispered in her ear. "If I hurt you I need you to tell me okay?" looking deep into her eyes she blinked and nodded slowly.

"Okay"

Getting into a comfortable position I reached between us and gently started stroking her folds again. Her eyes rolled up into her head as she fell back onto the pillows with a moan. As easy as possible I dipped my fingers in and out of her juices till she had started dripping with excitement. Moving my hips into position ready to enter her I slowly removed my fingers and guided the tip of the toy to her entrance.

"Remember just tell me okay?" I said as I kissed her again. Pressing my hips closer to hers the tip began inching its way into her cave.

A moment of minor resistance met me as she gasped from the sensation before the dildo entered with a slow pull. Her torso began jerking up off the bed as I began slowly making my way deeper still.

With a hiss like a cat I felt my fangs elongate as my jaw worked to resist biting her again. Instead I bit down on my lip leaving tiny puncture marks in it.

Her hips jerked off the bed as I inched my way further into her. Her arms flung up and wrapped around my back till her nails had begun digging into my skin, her legs that had been still for the first part had found themselves around my hips and were urging me further.

With one final push I was fully inside her. Gasping at the accomplishment I heard a deep throaty growl from beneath me. Looking into her eyes it seemed as though a spiral of yellow had spun through them, though when I looked again they were her lovely blue. Slowly I began moving my hips in a pulling and pushing motion till her body started convulsing.

We both had started panting like dogs when I noticed she had begun to plateau. Not wanting to lose the momentum

I looked in her eyes and with a hunting cat snarl I bared my fangs at her. Her own eyes widened in terror and I struck her neck again with my fangs making a final surge into her hips.

I could hear her crying out in pleasure and pain as I drank deeply for the first time from her. Her nails bit into my back like little claws and her hips rode me out till her body bucked three maybe four more times and finally collapsed in a heap of pleasure. Removing my fangs from her neck I carefully licked the stray droplets from the punctures and looked into her eyes. She looked sated beyond measure as her breathing began to slow down.

I don't know what made me do it, I don't know what was possibly going through my head. But I do know as she touched my skin with a caress so soft and genuine, I knew that she was the one for me. When our lips pressed together in the softest most wonderful moment I felt as though the world fell beneath my feet. I felt as though I was falling not in the bad way that you see in movies or reading any kind of book but the way it feels when the one that you love the most is holding you close and watching as though you are their whole world, their whole galaxy I looked deeply into her eyes and said the one thing that would change our fate for good.

"Move in with me."

Chapter 8

Chill

"What?!" my mouth dropped open in shock at Zoey's statement.

"I want you to move in with me. You don't have to answer right now but at least consider it. I've found the one whom my soul sings for and I know it is you." she leaned down and kissed me again. "You have woken me up Tara, you have given my life meaning again... you've made me happy."

Looking deep into her eyes I bit my lip. "I can think about it a bit?" I said uncertainty

Her eyes widened "of course! I don't want to pressure you at all. Take as much time as you need" she smiled softly "Here, let's get cleaned up first then we can get something to snack on, maybe watch a movie or as the kids say, netflix and chill." she giggled into my ear and kissed my neck. As she moved her hips back the toy slid out with a pop. Zoey sat up and removed the other end of it before setting it on the night stand.

Slowly getting up she wandered to the other door in the room and flicked on the light. I could hear the sound of running water echoing from the room. Shortly she wandered back out. "I've got a bath going if you wanna use it. I have to call Jeremy, I promised I would let him know when you woke up." walking back to me she gave me a swift kiss and grabbed a styrofoam cup from the table. As she walked to the door I watched the swing of her hips as she left and felt a stirring deep in my gut. Shaking my head I tenderly sat up and looked down between my legs. There was a pool of blood and the place she had bitten me earlier that looked weeks old already. Embarrassed I tossed my legs over the bed and walked to the bathroom.

The huge mirror over the clawfoot tub caught my eye, it had black scrolling around the frame with a treeline painted along the bottom. Leaning in I examined my neck on both sides and frowned. The left side where the intruder had given me a shot had welled up in a red patch but the right side had a bruise the size of my fist. The puncture wounds had sealed up but the skin had turned a purplish black color with yellow surrounding it. Shutting the water off I slipped into the tub grateful to be left alone for a moment.

She wants me to move in with her… what would I tell Jeremy and Tom? Would they think it was too fast? I mean I've only known her for about roughly a week if that. What if she…

I didn't even wanna think the last thought.

She would never intentionally hurt me. And thinking about it. I'm more happy here than I have been for a while…

I slid deeper into the tub and leaned my head back. I could hear Zoey talking on the phone through the door.

"I know Jeremy but she's fine if she wants to stay here for the night I have space in my bed… that's- FUCK YOU! ITS NONE OF YOUR GODDAMNED BUSINESS WHO SHE CHOOSES TO- …. Oh shut the hell up ya fairy. I'll let her know… yeah I sent a clean up crew to your place to put everything right. They left about an hour ago it seems. Gotta love text messages. Yeah it's fine we… we are fine. Yeah. Alright, goodnight Jeremy"

I heard a slurping noise like a straw trying to get the last bit of liquid from a cup. The banging of cabinets echoed through the apartment. Waiting on the hiss of a can of pop I frowned when it didn't happen. With a shrug I started washing my body with soap that smelled like a rainstorm. After finishing with my bath I got up and toweled myself off and slipped into the robe that was hanging off the back of the door.

Walking out into the hallway I saw Zoey's back to me with her head bent down. Creeping up behind her I heard a distinct noise of plastic rustling around. Her hand came down as she went to lean on the counter. Her nails had gotten considerably longer and turned into wicked looking points. Backing up slowly till I was at the entrance of the bedroom again I yelled out.

"Hey Zoey? Can I use this robe in the bathroom? I can't seem to find my underwear"

Best not to interrupt her while she is feeding…

A muffled voice yelled back "yeah of course go for it." not until I heard something hitting a trashbag did I wander out of the room again to see her bending into a cabinet under the sink.

"Um so- what did Jeremy say?" I asked looking around the kitchen.

Looking up from the sinks bottom she smiled. "Says to be careful around those lesbians, and if you want to stay the night you are an adult and can do what you want. Also if you need him just give him a ring or text him or Tom."

"Ah… okay… um, what are you doing?" Curiosity had gotten the better of me.

Her hand seemed to have frozen above where she was reaching, her eyes clouded for a split second. "Well… To be honest I was still thirsty. And if you had wanted to continue what we keep getting wrapped up in. I need to feed because if I take too much from you it could be really bad… so I've been getting a pint here and there while you rest to make sure that doesn't happen." looking at me her lips tightened slightly her eyes begging me to understand.

"Oh… well do you mind if I watch? I know that sounds weird but I've well I've never seen a vampire feed before." I said trying to play it off as no big deal.

Blinking fast she frowned and then snorted a laugh. "I

suppose that would be okay, I mean it's about as interesting as someone drinking water." grabbing something out from beneath the sink she kicked the door closed lightly and set 2 pint bags down on the counter. The blood was a deep rust color with little labels on the front declaring them to be O-negative and AB-Positive. "Since I'm snacking would you like some? Like... Food?" she added as my eyes widened at her offer.

"Oh no I'm okay but if you have maybe pop or some kind of juice I wouldn't mind." I flushed with embarrassment at my own tongue.

Zoey walked to the fridge and opened it up looking at me with her eyebrow cocked up. "Pick your poison." walking back to the counter with a smile playing on her lips I scurried off to the fridge and grabbed myself an off brand brown pop. Watching her out of the corner of my eye, I cracked the can open. Bringing it to my lips I saw her shiver as her fangs began descending and turn into long points. Her eyes took on the purple color once again as her skin turned pale as a ghost. With a strike like a cobra she had the bag in her mouth with her fangs dug deeply into it. She grabbed the other bag and walked to the couch and plopped down completely at ease as if it was an everyday thing that happens. I watched her place the extra blood bag on the side table and with her free hand she patted the spot next to her with a smile.

Quickly I walked to sit next to her as she scooched closer till our sides were flush with one another. The noise of a straw draining came from the bag as she took the last remnants of the blood from it. Giving her the side eye again I watched as she tossed the bag on the table and turned to look at me.

Her hand had made its way around me and the long nails had started playing with my hair. Shifting in my seat a little bit I noticed a small splatter of blood on her cheek. Lifting my hand up I wiped it away with my thumb, her eyes followed it as I placed it on her lips. Her tongue darted out and licked the droplet as she smiled.

"What do you wanna watch?" she asked as looked at me with lust. Pulling my thumb into her mouth she lightly bit my finger between her teeth.

"Um I-" the sharp little jolts from her teeth raced through my hands and went directly between my legs making me want more. My breath hissed out through my mouth in a rush as she trailed kisses from my hand up my arm.

"C-can we just skip- mmm. Skip Netflix and j-just oh my god" her mouth had made it to my ear as she slowly nibbled on the lobe. I heard a giggle escape her lips as her hand found my breast through the robe.

"you wanna just what my darling?" she laughed, squeezing lightly on my chest.

With a moan my head fell back on the couch as she climbed into my lap and began undulating her body into mine. My eyes trailed down her beautiful naked form as my hands reached up to grip her ass.

Zoey leaned down into my ear and whispered lightly. "I have a new game we can play. Come with me." as she climbed off of me she grabbed my hand and led me into the bedroom once more.

Chapter 9

Bold move

I had really considered moving in with Zoey. Not just because the sex was phenomenal but because she made me feel like a new person. I checked the clock for the umpteenth time today as I packed the rest of my meager belongings into 4 boxes I had scrounged up. Jeremy and Tom were at work today but said if I ever needed anything that I just had to knock.

Zoey hadn't hidden her excitement at all when I told her yes. In fact she brought me to a ritzy furniture outlet to let me pick whatever out for her- our home. We spent hours there and she took me out to eat. She pushed her food around to make it seem like she had eaten more than a few bites and I was surprised when she ordered extra garlic butter on her chicken. She laughed when I voiced my concerns. I love hearing her laugh.

The night was almost ruined though when I felt a sharp twisting pain in my gut. It nearly floored me when we were walking back home. I am glad she was there to help carry me back to the apartment, I simply played it off as food poisoning when she laid me in the bed that night with a cold rag on my forehead.

Looking at the calendar on the wall a jolt shot through my system in just one day I would be 20 years old! It amazed me how fast my life here had flown by. Looking at the clock again I heard a knock on the door.

"Tara! Its me! Open up!" Zoey had taken to yelling at the door. Gently I opened it as she bustled in with her arms full. She had a box wrapped in gaudy bow and thrust it at me.

"I know it's early but Jeremy told me your birthday is tomorrow and I wanted to get you something." the box wiggled and I heard a whimper coming from inside it. My curiosity perked up as the box moved again.

Gently pulling the bow apart a little snout started sniffing at the opening. I grabbed the edges of a box to reveal a beautiful white dog.

"He's a great pyrenees husky mix. He will probably get as big as you but he is currently 10 weeks old" Zoey said laughing. The puppy tilted his head towards me and I noticed he had little blonde tips on his ears and snout.

"So he's gonna get huge?" I asked looking at Zoey.

"Yeah they said he would be between 110-130 lbs when he's fully grown if not more 'cause of the husky in him."

"Hmm... well since he's gonna get so big can we call him... Atlas? Cause he could probably carry the world on his back if he tried" looking at him he cocked his head to the side and wagged his tail a little bit.

With a laugh Zoey said "Of course! I think Atlas is the perfect name for him. Come on let's get him all dolled up." grabbing the leash and harness out of the box she helped me slip it onto his torso.

"I have my stuff packed so we can stop by home before we go out that way we don't have to come back today. It's in the room." gently I tugged the lease and Atlas looked at me and started trotting close by my side.

I stopped at the door and slipped the leash holder on the handle. Picking up two boxes Zoey had followed and grabbed the last ones. Grabbing the leash off the handle Atlas wandered next to my side without having to even be tugged.

"Good boy!" I said looking down at him. He peeked up at me and wagged his tail a few times before concentrating on the stairs. Zoey passed my opposite side and unlocked the door with her free hand and opened it up for me. Placing my boxes down we walked back onto the stairwell and outside to the sidewalk.

Zoey bounded up next to me and held my hand. As we walked Atlas looked around with little interest at passing things. Even when a stray cat passed us he completely ignored it and stayed by our side.

Zoey leaned close to my ear and whispered. "I love how much control you have over him with that thing. Think we could get me one to play with? Oh! I also got you this!" pulling out a box from her pocket she giggled and pecked my cheek lightly. I felt my face heat up and flush with a wide grin.

Opening the box revealed a beautiful silver pendant with a stone on it connected with little silver clamps holding it in place.

"Its beautiful!" Taking it out of the box she put it around my neck delicately.

Atlas snorted as though he understood what was said between us.

We had walked three maybe four blocks before we had made it to the pet boutique. Seeing all the little collars and outfits I oogled at the rhinestone collar on display. The price was astronomical!

"Um Zoey... I can't afford any of this stuff... i just have the part time job at the-" Zoey pressed her lips to mine to silence me.

"Don't worry baby I got it. Anything you want it's yours. Think of it as your birthday present add on." grinning at me she went to the counter and ordered a twenty two pound bag of food, a dog bed the size of a dining table, several squeaky toys and a matching leash and collar combo with an ID tag stating his name and our address with a phone number.

The total came to more than my last pay check and I felt myself go pale from it. She grabbed the bags as I protested it about being too much and we walked back out to the street.

When we got back to our apartment I took Atlas's harness off and replaced it with the deep navy collar we had gotten instead. It brought out the light blue of his eyes beautifully. Zoey set up his bed in the living room and he wandered gratefully to it and plopped down.

"He is the most chill puppy I have ever seen! Why isn't he more... I don't know... active?"

"Well we did get back from a walk and it is a new environment. He could just be tired" she said with a shrug.

A few hours passed as we watched a few tv shows when I saw that the clock said 11:45 pm.

"Jesus it's already that late? We didn't even get to play tonight" I said with a pout. Zoey looked over at me with a smile.

"Oh baby the night is still young!" she swung her legs over my hips and began kissing me deeply. My face started feeling extremely hot again as I looked into her eyes.

I noticed a frown forming on her brow. "Tara? Are you okay? You feel feverish" her cool hand touched my forehead gently.

"I feel fine I just have too many clothes on for my liking." my skin had begun to prickle with anticipation and my face flushed. Grabbing my shirt I began tugging it over my head.

"Tara! You're not looking too good baby maybe we should hold off. Just... just so you can rest a bit." Zoey's voice had shot up a few octaves at the end.

"I told you I feel fine! I'm just really hot right now is all." my skin had begun itching more and more as a burning sensation started rocketing through me. Looking at my arms my hair had raised straight up. Ignoring the sensation I grabbed Zoey's face in my hands and began kissing her. My mouth felt as though I had grown an extra set of molars. I felt Zoey relax into me as she began kissing me back. Licking her lips I moved down to her neck and started nibbling her neck.

"OUCH!" She exclaimed. Jerking my head back I looked at where I had bitten her and saw a huge red welt forming where I had somehow punctured the skin. Her blood was almost black in color and I smelled rust. Her hand flew up and touched the ooze and looked into my eyes.

"What the hell Tara- your... oh my god your eyes!"

"What about my eyes?" I asked confused. I heard the clock in the living room chime saying that it was now midnight. My skin began burning and itching more as the pain in my stomach doubled me over. I heard Zoey scream my name before I felt nothing but pain.

I had propped myself up with my hands and saw the skin bubbling and moving as though I had worms crawling beneath them. I could hear Zoey screaming and trying to touch me. A guttural noise escaped my lips in an almost barking growl. I felt a whimper escape as I moaned "help me." My body began to violently shaking as I toppled off the bed onto the floor. It felt as though my skin was eating me from the inside out. My eyes rolled into the back of my head and I was twitching violently.

I felt the hair on my arms growing my skin had grown super sensitive as more deep brown almost black hair sprouted all over my body. My face felt like it was stretching as every bone in my body snapped and regrew longer. Falling to the ground fully I saw my fingers shrinking before being overtaken by more hair.

I think I had blacked out for a moment because when I had awoken I noticed the bright colors in the room had dimmed almost to gray. Only a few colors had remained the deep reds, yellows, and blues. I looked around in confusion and tried to stand up my legs buckled under me and I face planted into the carpet. Zoey was backed into the corner holding the very same metal bat I had used towards her. Her lips were moving and all I heard was a muffled noise like she was talking through a tunnel.

I concentrated on her words trying to decipher them but all I heard was "good doggy, nice doggy. Go play."

I shook my head a few times trying to clear it, the smells of the room overpowered everything else. The scent coming from the person in front of me was mouthwatering, her face had screwed up into a defensive anger. She swung the bat wildly when I lifted my head, I could hear the metal whistle through the air as it barely missed my snout. Her fear laced all around me sending a shiver down my spine, a low growl bubbled up from the pit of my stomach as she swung again.

Looking around the room I noticed the windows showing the bright full moon off. My hair prickled in anticipation as I felt my muscles tense, the fur upon my neck stood straight up as a wild thought flew in my brain. *I need meat.*

Taking a few steps backwards, I raced past the girl and flew across the room in a bound that sent me right through the window from the second story. The ground came rushing up at me as I landed with a loud bone jarring thump, but I didn't care. Moving my legs as fast as I could manage I sprinted forward towards the alleyway and lept over a homeless man who had curled into a box. My claws clicked into the sidewalk as my legs powered me through the streets. Late night drivers honked as I sped past in a whirl of fur. The tantalising smells of the city made my stomach rumble in anticipation. A cat streaked past causing me its back arched as its tail bushed up in defense. Ahead of me I saw a park where the whisper of winds through the trees ruffled the delicate leaves.

I smelled a mix of dirt and blood through the air that I couldn't resist checking out. I followed the scent closely with my nose pressed upon the earth till a popping noise crossed my path. Looking up I saw a man standing over a body with a gun. I felt a deep rumbling growl bubble up from my chest,

63

the smell of blood was driving me crazy. The man looked up and saw me, terror flashed across his face as he raised the gun to point it towards me.

I lept at him as another series of pops echoed across the park, a burning sensation skimmed my right shoulder as I tackled him to the ground and ripped his throat out. His body began convulsing in on itself as my claws dug deep into his exposed skin. The last thought I had before I blacked out was how delicious it all was.

Chapter 10

Destruction

Zoey

Looking at the place that Tara had once stood I braced myself against the wall for support. The room had started spinning out of control to where I had to put my head between my knees just to gasp in a breath. Looking at the broken window with a shaky hand I pulled out my phone and called Jeremy.

"Hullo?" his sleep riddled voice answered after three rings.

"Jeremy-" my voice was raspy and coarse "Tara... she's gone." the tone of my voice must have woken him up fully cause all I heard after that was shouting from the other side as he tried to wake Tom.

"We'll be there in a second. DON'T YOU FUCKING MOVE!" as the line went dead my breath started coming out in wimpers till the tears started rolling down my face causing my shoulders to shake and convulse.

I heard the door bang open as two sets of footsteps pounded through the house till they reached my door where Jeremy and Tom burst forth into the room. Tom ran to my side as Jeremy began firing off a barrage of questions at me. After I explained what had happened with Tara the shaking started up again to where I started moaning horribly.

Tom looked at Jeremy with wide eyes and quietly asked "Did you know that she was like you?"

After one hour and a plan of action all of us were out the door ready to catch the beast that was now Tara. Jeremy would use his heightened senses while Tom kept an eye out for him in case he started changing too. I was on puppy duty, with Atlas hooked up to his leash I led him down the stairs with my aluminum bat in tow. If I can't reason with Tara then my bat will have to do the talking.

Trodding down the sidewalk Atlas's tail began to bristle up slightly at a scent he caught. Following closely with him he led me directly to Highbridge Park where right under a streetlight was a very large red splash in the grass that had seeped onto the sidewalk. Grabbing my phone from my pocket I quickly dialed Tom's number when he answered on the first ring.

"There is a lot of blood over here, I'm at Highbridge park next to-" looking around a little bit for a landmark "the baseball field closest to the swimming pool. Hurry your ass up." hanging up Atlas led me past the stain following a very long smear to a severed hand that looked as though it had been chewed on by a very large dog.

The hair on the back of my neck started to stand up when I bent down to examine it. A deep rumbling growl permeated the silence of the park. As I lifted my head up to look for the source of the noise a huge towering brown wolf was staring back at me, teeth pulled back in a highly aggressive manner with blood dripping off of its muzzle.

"Tara? Tara it's me Zoey." Putting my hands up in an I surrender position the wolf's eyes darted between the baseball bat and Atlas. Her hackles raised up as she became prepared to spring at me. Within two seconds the giant 150lb wolf had launched itself just as I had grabbed the bat and swung it into her with all my might right into the side of its head causing her to fall to the ground in a heap of fur and legs.

"TARA!" Tom and Jeremy came from the opposite direction running towards me. Looking down at the massive beast at my feet they shared a look between each other and grabbed her by the legs to take her back home.

Chapter 11
Reveal

—◦◦⟨◦⟩◦◦—

Tara

The first thing that I noticed when I came too was a pounding in my head that felt as though a jackhammer was destroying my cranium. Gently opening my eyes I noticed that I was in Zoey an my room, with the muted light from the bathroom calling me like a siren. As easy as possible I slowly raised myself up to a seated position and lowered my feet off the edge of the bed till the balls of my feet touched the cold hardwood. Taking a deep breath I raised myself up to a semi standing position and began shuffling around the room gripping objects along the way to keep my balance.

After using the facilities I started hearing voices coming from the living room. I could distinctly make out three people chatting quietly.

Zoey

"So when will she be changing again and how do I need to

prepare for it?" I asked both Jeremy and Tom "cause I don't know about you but coming by windows for this place is a rather pretty penny."

"I know the feeling" Tom gave me a knowing look "when Jeremy first changed he tore up my brand new mattress and futon. I had just got that shit delivered from IKEA, didn't even have it assembled yet." Jeremy poked Tom in the ribs angrily.

"I've told you a thousand times that I was sorry!" with an exasperated sigh Jeremy looked at me.

"My advice Zoey, put her in a bathroom or something that can't be broken out of easily and make sure you bar up any and all exits or we may get a repeat of murders in the park. We are just lucky it wasn't hard to clean up, she kinda ate most of him so not nearly as much mess to remove."

I heard the toilet flush in the bathroom and looked between Tom and Jeremy.

"I think you should let me break the news to her… if she has any questions after I'll send her your way ok?"

Mutely both of them rose up and gave me a quick hug and peck on the cheek before exiting. Taking a few deep breaths I started walking to our bedroom and gently opened the door. Tara was standing slouched against the bathroom door frame as though she had gotten a bout of the flu and was gonna keel over on the spot.

Rushing to her side I swung her arm over my neck lightly and stabilized her. "Tara are you okay? Did you get sick?"

Tara

I wasn't sick was I? I felt weak my stomach was off and my head was pounding, maybe I am sick.

"I had to pee but I got dizzy on the way back to bed. That food must have really messed me up bad." I said trying to smile but only succeeding with a grimace. As Zoey led me back to bed I noticed the concern on her porcelain features.

"I'll be fine Zoey just got food poisoning is all." her eyebrows shot up past her bangs as she gazed at me.

"You think you have food poisoning?" she blinked a few times before continuing. "Tara, sweety you… well you aren't human. You are a werewolf or lupin or whatever you wanna call it. You… you killed someone tonight."

Frowning I tried to recall what I did last night. "All I remember is coming in here right around midnight and passing out cold. Wait what do you mean I'm not human? Of course I'm human I-" the rest of her sentence whisked by my thoughts "I couldn't have killed anyone! I was here I passed out on the floor cause I felt sick!" Zoey's eyes took on a very sad and concerned look to where I felt immediately ill. "Oh god, I killed someone."

A cold lump had formed in my stomach as bile started rising up my throat. I jerked over the side of the bed and felt the vomit expel itself from my body. Zoey's hissing curse came as she jumped out of the way of my sick. I heard her running around grabbing something when a cold rag was pressed to my forehead as she rubbed my back gently. Her comforting voice was like an anchor holding me into the real world soothing my head.

After what seemed like forever my stomach had emptied itself of all the contents and I fell back onto the pillows. I could feel the darkness creeping up around me again as I tried fighting it I locked eyes with Zoey once more before I passed out again.

<u>Zoey</u>

It took me an hour to scrub the floors clean after Tara had gotten ill, I didn't mind cleaning it up however, I mean she didn't do it on purpose. Walking to the shower I flipped on the water and ran it till steam rolled out of the bathroom like a cloud. I began stripping my sick coaked clothing off and undid my hair from atop my head letting the mahogany waves roll down my breasts.

Looking at myself in the mirror I noticed right under my eyes deep almost bruise like marks were starting to puff out at my touch. I knew I would need to get fresh blood soon or I would look more gaunt than normal.

Stepping into the shower I looked at the removable shower head massaging tool and smiled to myself privately. Peeking out to make sure that I closed the door properly I removed the shower head from its holder and tested the water lightly along my chest. The water being so hot left a wonderful stinging sensation with a trail of welts behind. Grabbing the faucet knob I turned a little more cold water on enough to where the welts weren't an angry red anymore at least.

Sitting on the little ledge where I normally shave my legs and other places I turned the faucet to deep tissue massage mode where it felt like little pellets shooting out of the head. Leaning back and getting comfortable I slowly traced the water along my breast as my other hand went down south between my legs. My folds were already soaking before I had a chance to even begin touching. Slowly I inserted two fingers into myself and began rubbing my thumb back and forth gently to the swaying of my hips.

I began trailing the shower head down my body till it was just right above my belly. My mind wandered to early last week when Tara and I were rubbing against each others legs in a frenzied dry humping. I could feel pleasure from the memory uncoiling from my stomach till my fingers started matching my hips in pace. Popping them out of myself I brought the shower head downward till it was right between my legs in a pleasurable massaging pattern. My eyes began rolling to the back of my head as I started grinding myself against the head of the shower.

My legs kicked out to the sides as I began grinding harder against it as my pointer finger teased my clit lightly till I was squirming for more. A slow moan escaped my lips and I started to swivel my hips back and forth trying to find the correct angle to get myself off. Closing my eyes I leaned my head back and let my mind wander through my favorite times with Tara.

The door opened a crack as someone came wandering in. Frowning I peeked out the shower door to see Tara with her back to me removing the underwear I had put on her, slowly I placed the shower head back to where it belongs when warm arms snaked around my waist. A hand as hot as a fever began tracing down my body till it reached my pubic hair.

"Tara... you're still sick you need to go to bed."

Her hand continued further through the light smattering of curls till it found my clit engorged still from my unfinished shower playtime. A rumbling growl of a question purred from behind me. Almost asking permission to continue.

"I-I guess if you're feeling better" I stammered out as she stroked the hair lightly.

With speed like a hunting cat she flipped me till my arms were braced against the wall and my legs were spread wide as though I were getting frisked. I heard a thump as she sat down to her knees as I was turning to look her mouth had latched there on my sweet spot and was sucking the very life out of me till my knees were shaking.

Her hands had snaked up till they were cupping both hips and pushing me deeper into her mouth. Her tongue felt almost flat like a dogs as it played between my privates and caused my knees to bend as she went deeper and deeper into me.

As fast as she had started I felt her jerk my hips up till I was bent fully to the ground. I noticed the blue dildo hanging between her legs as I mentally prepared myself to be entered from behind she found my entrance and slammed into me filling me up like a glove.

I cried out at the force as she repeatedly slammed into me, a low whimper escaped my lips as she held my hips tighter to her body. A deep rumbling growl started to bubble from her throat as she picked up speed. An almost animalistic thrusting pressed her body closer to mine till her breasts were pressed to my shoulders. I felt myself plateauing till I felt her heated labored breath on the nape of my neck. With a final slam I felt her mouth grab my nape as she bit down hard enough to draw blood and cause me to orgasm in a wave of pleasurable pain. My hips began shaking as she pulled the well used dildo out of me. The water had turned icy causing me to hiss in discomfort. Grabbing the handle I quickly turned it off and spun to look at her.

The first thing I noticed were her eyes had taken on the golden glow once again. My hand shot up to my neck where she had bitten me and I felt a sticky ooze dripping out from the puncture wounds. Her nostrils flared as she took in my scent, her body quivering in anticipation. She took a slow step forward and before I knew it I was pressed against the shower wall pinned there by her once again.

"Tara? Tara I need a minute" her mouth captured mine as I started to protest. Her arms wrapped around me as her nails dug furrows into my back. Breaking her mouth away from mine I hissed louder as the pain sent itself up my spine.

"Tara! STOP!" her greedy mouth moved to my neck once again and started nibbling at the vein on my neck. I felt my eyes turn to their dark purple color as my fangs elongated to sharp points. She wasn't stopping her pursuit, so I did the only thing I could think of.

Grabbing her thick hair I yanked her head up and bit her neck as hard as I could till she yelped and leapt backwards causing us to slip and fall in a heap on the tiled floor. Both her and my blood leaked onto the wet floor as we scrambled to get away from each other. My back pressed against the bathroom door I threw the lightswitch off in hopes that she wouldn't be able to see.

Still in the shower Tara's eyes glowered angrily at me, shining with the reflection of an animal.

"Tara, sweetheart?" a deep growl answered me. "Tara please honey, come back to me. This isn't you, you can fight this. I know you would never hurt me. Please just come back to me." my pleading went on for what seemed like hours till her eyes closed fully and I saw her form droop to the ground like a sack of bricks. Rushing to her side I checked for a pulse and was surprised at how strong it was beneath my fingers. Slowly I scooped her up and moved her to the bedroom where I removed the toy from her, tossing it into the bedside drawer I locked it tight. A strong smell of musk saturated the air in the bedroom when I smelled my skin I was covered in it.

Tossing on my robe i grabbed my phone and called up Jeremy once again to tell him what happened.

Tara

My skin was burning like a fire was trapped under it, my neck and back felt as though I had deep tissue bruising. I could feel a feverish cold sweat beading my brow as though I had gotten sick. Frowning I slowly opened my eyes to see the bedside lamp was on, and Zoey standing over me with gauze bandages and a glass of water in each hand. My mouth had immediately become a desert wasteland with a foul aftertaste burning my throat.

Trying to swallow I looked into her eyes and noticed they were the deep purple with dark bruising under them as though she hadn't slept in a week.

"Hey-" my voice rasped out to a coughing fit. Trying to sit up I felt a tugging on my arms and legs, looking at my wrists I noticed I had been loosely tied to the bedpost with what seemed to be a mishmash of silk scarves. "Z-Zoey why am I tied to our bed? Can you let me up?" my voice was still hoarse.

"That depends Tara." her voice sounded like an icepick. "Are you gonna attack me again?"

"Attack?" my eyes trailed up and down her body and I noticed half healed bruises and cuts all along her hip line and up her ribs to where her neck was bandaged heavily. I could feel my eyes widen in horror and shame. *What the fuck did I do to her!?*

"I… I attacked you? I did all of that?" I saw her body droop slightly as though she was relieved.

"You didn't mean to do it, your- well I spoke with Jeremy and he said it sounded like your wolf was walking around doing what it did…" she walked to my feet and untied the slipknot from my ankles and up above where my hands were. Clenching and unclenching my hands I noticed deep red welts had formed along my wrists where I had apparently tugged hard at my makeshift bonds.

Zoey had still not touched me, even while removing the scarves her hand hadn't brushed mine.

"I'm sorry Zoey, I didn't know, I would never hurt you on purpose. Please… please believe me." my voice started hiccuping as tears pooled in my eyes.

Zoey sat down next to me and pulled me into a tight hug. "Tara no please don't cry! I'm just worried about you. I'm not mad" her hands were petting my hair gently as though I was made of glass.

Once my tears subsided she grabbed a tissue off the nightstand and gave it to me. "Come on blow your nose and dry your eyes. Here take some of this." she gave me the glass of water with two little white oval pills. "Its headache medicine I'm sure your head is pounding, let me have a look at your neck"

Turning my head to take the pills I felt her cool fingers brush my vein as she wrapped a bandage around what I assume were her puncture wounds she had made. The smell

77

of her skin had changed slightly, she had more of a musky odor mixed with her natural private smell.

Mine a voice flew through my head and sent shivers down my spine. Zoey looked up at me in confusion.

"Did that hurt?"

"Oh uh, no just… no. What else did Jeremy say?"

With a frown she looked back to my neck to adjust the bandages before speaking.

"He said you will have very strong urges that you will need to control both physical and mental, it will be very difficult at first but he is willing to help you."

"So Jeremy is… he's like me?"

"Yeah he is, he said the first change can happen between 20-25 years old. Though you seem to be on the early spectrum. But since you are the first female in about three generations it's to be expected. He didn't want to scare you if it turned out it wouldn't happen. That's why your parents came. They apparently knew what you were and were gonna auction you off to the top alpha male of the cult. Where you would have been impregnated and forced to have child after child till a new alpha arose where you would be given to them like a slab of meat." Zoey's voice turned sour at the last part. "But that's why I'm here for you. I volunteered to keep you safe and happy because I felt a connection with you." her eyes met mine and I felt a burning sensation rocket through my chest till it settled between my legs. Shifting uncomfortably my sense of smell seemed to triple, her supple skin was giving off a heated musky odor that was all **MINE**. My mouth had filled up with drool as a thought of her lying naked on the bed sent more heated jolts through me.

Her forehead scrunched up as her lips pursed in an unhappy manner.

"Lay back on the bed Tara." her voice had gone commanding.

With a frown I did as I was told "what's wrong?" her hands had grabbed mine as she tied me back on the bed. "Zoey? What are you-" my breath caught in my throat as a shooting pain corsed through my spine causing me to jacknife upward. My skin was on fire as my arms started twitching. Closing my eyes tightly my hands clenched as I tried to concentrate on my breathing. My legs began to flail wildly till Zoey caught them and held them down with the pressure of a car.

One last shiver spiked my body till I sagged into the pillows and looked down at her. "What was that?"

"You almost started changing, what were you thinking about before I told you to lay down?"

Shifting around my thighs rubbed together lightly sending shivers up my spine.

"well um… I was thinking of you honestly. And how you look when I'm between your legs…" a flush of embarrassment heated my cheeks till I was sure they were bright red. Zoey's eyes widened slightly till a small smile played on her lips.

"Really now? Well too bad you're all tied up in knots." her hands quickly tied each leg to a bedpost till I was spread eagled in front of her. Her eyes trailed down my body till she caught sight of my private area where an amused smile settled upon her lips.

"Oh baby what I wouldn't give to bite you right here." her fingernails dragged lightly up my leg following my vein till she stopped right below my pubic hair line. Her eyes became glossy and hooded as she licked her lips lightly before she blinked and frowned.

"I am gonna untie you, I need to get some food in me so I don't kill you, cause right now baby, I could drain you dry."

"You won't drain me, I'll stop you before you have a chance to. I'll say your name or something." looking at her with a primal passion I let myself relax back onto the pillows and wiggled my hips seductively. "Please? I want you to. I want you to be in control." I didn't realize I had started holding my breath till she slowly climbed onto the bed between my legs. Her eyes had taken on their deep purple color as she slowly dipped her head down.

"At some point, you will have to stop me." before I could even nod her fangs shot into my leg and began drinking deeply causing me to cuss loudly at the ceiling. I started pulling hard on my bonds again as her hand snaked up my other thigh till it pressed on my groin holding me down on the bed, her thumb roamed through my pubic hair till it found a sweet spot that caused me to buck wildly under her.

A snarl ripped through my throat as though a beast was uncurling from me. When her fingers made their way down between my legs to my folds my body lifted uncontrollably off the bed, yanking at the bonds once again. My head lolled back as her fingers butterflied through my labia and around my clitoris. A moaning whimper escaped between my teeth as she slid two delicate fingers into me and made a come hither motion. My senses were on fire, I could feel a deep burning pressure building in me as she continued her exploration of my body. My heart pounded as though I was a marathoner finishing a race. My breathing became ragged as she sped her fingers faster to where I cried out in a pitiful howl to the sky. My hips rocketed off the bed till she slowed to a stop. She slowly removed her fangs from my leg and licked the holes closed where she slid her fingers from me and snaked her tongue out to taste my juices.

The deep bruising under her eyes had started to fade as did the cuts and bruises along her body. Slowly she undid my bonds from my hands and ankles and curled into me with a satisfied sigh. Hugging her closely I drifted off into sleep next to her.

Chapter 12
Nightmares

~~∽∿◦⊙⟋⟍⊙◦∿∽~~

Zoey

My dreams always started the same, always after I feed. Im sitting alone on the beach, no older than about four or five. Just burrowing deeper in the sand when a dark cloud covers the sun and darkens the whole beach. All the adults leave and I'm still just digging into the sand. When I look up a tall man in victorian era clothing is standing over me and his teeth all of them were like needles as he grabbed my by the throat and ripped it out to taste my blood. That's when I usually wake up screaming.

This morning was no different. My eyes burst open and holding onto me was none other than Tara, the look of utter concern on her face as she tried to shake me awake. Reaching up my own hands I grasped hers lightly to settle her down. My breathing slowed as my sputtery heart returned to just one beat a minute rather than three.

"I'm okay" I said weakly as I gasped for breath. Her hands held mine tightly as her lips pressed to mine.

"Do you want to talk about it?" Tara's voice seemed warped in a half slowed down bark and her normal pitch. Her eyes were falling to half mast again as she gazed at me. Her face seemed longer than normal as her eyes had a familiar yellow gold swivel wisp through them. I noticed her nostrils flare outward slightly as her head tilted to the side.

Ever since she let me take control last night she hasn't left my side even though she's half asleep and the wolf is oddly active.

"No I'm sure, just another bad dream. Go back to sleep beautiful." petting her hair lightly I kissed her forehead and nuzzled back next to her comfortably till we were flush once again.

Early the next morning I woke up to a noise coming from the kitchen where the smell of bacon wafted into the room. Slowly getting up I wandered into the bathroom and grabbed my robe hanging from the hook on the bathroom door. It was one of my favorite ones, a beautiful teal color with black mandala print all over it. The silk lightly brushed my ankles, looking in the mirror I noticed the bruising had disappeared from under my eyes leaving them shiny and bright. Swishing my way out the door I wandered into the kitchen where Tara had set out 2 plates on the bar, a reusable plastic cup was sitting by one of the plates with a white and red striped straw poked out of the top.

Peeking under the lid I noticed a viscous red liquid sloshing around, taking a tentative sip I felt my eyes change to their deep purple color. Sitting down at the place setting I watched Tara dance around the kitchen to unheard music. As she spun around she froze noticing me for the first time, quickly she pulled her earbuds out and I could hear faint pop music playing from them.

"Hey, I was a bit hungry, do you want any?" She gave me a tentative smile as she reached up above in the cabinet for some spices.

"Yes please that sounds good. Just one egg scrambled please." She then walked over to the fridge and grabbed the dozen eggs off the shelf and grabbed one before placing the carton back onto the rack. Walking to the stove she cracked the egg in a bowl with the three other yokes she had previously opened and began whisking like a mad woman till they were fully blended. Smiling over at me she dumped the goop into the heated pan to where they started sizzling delicately.

As she placed the used bowl in the sink she turned the water on to fill it up. Swinging back over to the stove she finished the eggs off with salt, pepper, and paprika. Bringing the hot pan over to the plates she dished out the food and brought the bacon that was sitting on the counter and placed them down next to the eggs, placing the pan back onto the stove and went to sit down next to me. Tasting the eggs first they were fluffy and fresh, the flavor played on my tongue lightly. I noticed out of the corner of my eye that Atlas was sitting quietly by my feet begging for food. Slipping him a piece of bacon he eagerly chomped it down with a wag of his tail.

After a wonderful breakfast Tara walked to the bedroom with Atlas close by her side. Cleaning up the dishes that were left in the sink and on the stove I tossed them in the dishwasher to go through a cycle. Sauntering into the bedroom after Tara I slowly untied my robe tantalizingly showing off my goodies.

Sliding onto the bed I posed in a come to me position with my hand on my knee while propping myself up on my other elbow. I heard the sinks water running with the sound of teeth being brushed, after about a minute the water shut off and Tara came out buttoning up her work shirt. On her third button she looked up and noticed me, her eyes spiraled with yellow as a slow grin spread across her face.

"Like what you see?" I asked suggestively as I wiggled my hips.

"I Love what I see. But I do have to go to work to help pay for the window I broke." Her eyes trailed down my body and paused at the v between my legs as a slow moan escaped her lips.

"You don't need to work baby, my paintings cover all the cost of everything and then some. Plus I need you here for…" moving my hand off my knee I began trailing it down my stomach and pausing at the dusting of hair I had there. "Inspiration."

Tara shivered lightly as she watched my hand slide lower as I played with myself gently. Her eyes had taken on a deep golden glow, when I reached my genitals she let another moan escape.

"Fine." her hands gripped both sides of her shirt opening and ripped till all the buttons she had just done had either flew across the room or were hanging by a thread. Slipping her pants down she tore off her bra and underwear and I was under her in a heartbeat. Her lips searched till she found mine and our heated breath mixed between us. The light smell of mint wafted from her as she made her way to my ear and nibbled the lobe there, as her mouth moved downward she began sucking on my neck and down my collar bone. When her mouth made it to my pierced nipple my body jerked up into hers, her tongue played gently with the ring there as one hand grasped my other breast and her other snaked between my legs lightly tugging the hair down below. With gentle tugs on the scattered curls nearly sent me over the edge so soon.

She removed her mouth from the one side with a gentle pop and moved to my other nipple while switching hands to play between my legs again. My body felt as though electricity was going through my skin, as her mouth moved downward she paused at my bellybutton to look into my eyes. The light from her eyes made me feel as though I was front and center with high beams, the glowing bubbled excitement in my stomach that shot directly to my groin.

"I'm going to devour you." Her voice had become warped to a deep gravellike growl that washed over me. As she slid further down my body I peered down at her as her eyes closed and her tongue twisted out into me. I noticed her tongue had become flat and resembled more of a dog's tongue, her nostrils flared out wide as she began lapping at the folds between my legs eagerly. My head lolled backwards as her hands slid up my rear till she had pulled me closer to her mouth burrowing deeper into me.

When I tried to squirm her hands tightened around me and pulled me further to her mouth as she swiveled that damn tongue in and out of me. One of her hands flew to my stomach as the other one caressed its way down my back completely sandwiching me. Looking at her hand I noticed the hair on her arms slowly standing on end, as she pressed her mouth closer into me I felt her mouth vibrate as though her lips were quivering.

"Baby? Are you oka-" her lips sucked my labia in between her teeth till she was nibbling lightly successfully cutting off my sentence. Her eyes had turned to slits while her pupils engorged to twice their normal size. Her tongue dug deeper into me lapping at my flowing juices. Her nails had grown to small little points and were caressing my stomach leaving little trails where the skin raised up from the contact. Tara's legs had begun scissoring against themselves as she was trying to ignore her own pleasure to get me off.

"Come up here." my hands went to hers and began pulling till she was braced above me, her mouth was covered in wetness from me. Her tongue came out and licked her lips off, it had turned a light purple color with dark black spots on it like a chow chow, while her teeth had lengthened and sharpened to doglike points. A purring growl escaped through her lips as she leaned down to my mouth and nibbled my lips. With a gasp my body arched into hers pressing our bodies together.

My hands trailed down her shoulders till I made it to her hips where I circled the bones there sending shivers up her spine. Reaching over to the bedside table I unlocked the top drawer and grabbed the well loved dildo out of the depths within.

"Do you wanna be in control or shall I?" I asked playfully with a smile. A guttural growl escaped her as she tried to talk past all of her new teeth. "No answer? Alright then. Get on all fours bitch!" I smacked her ass hard enough to cause her to yelp.

"H-hey!" her voice was still warped and sounded like gravel. Gently she slipped off of me and rolled into position, eyeing the toy speculatively.

Slowly I traced the toy down my body as she watched me in lustful anticipation, when it reached between my legs I grinned at her. Slowly slipping it into my folds I moaned with pleasure as it filled me up wonderfully. Sitting up on my knees I wobbled over behind her and looked down at her offering, she had her milky white ass presented upward to me while her elbows were braced onto the bed. Her genitals were engorged to what looked like the point of pain, her labia and clitorus were soaked with need. Slowly I got into position behind her and pressed the tip of the toy into her opening, gently circling the area around it. Pressing lightly a moan echoed around the room as she pressed her rear closer to me, I noticed her legs had started shaking from pleasure.

"You like that don't you? Well if you are a good girl I may just let you do this to me." her eyes lit up like christmas at my sentence.

Pressing it further into her I backpedaled just a little before thrusting fully, her body bucked under me as she tried getting closer to the base. As her hips pressed harder into me I began driving wildly into her. The musky scent had started perfuming the room with its thick sweet smell that called to me on a primal level causing my hips to work faster into her. Tara's skin was on fire compared to mine as I bent down closer so our bodies were fully touching. My breasts began hitting her back as I hung on for dear life as we bucked and fucked each other wildly.

With one fluid motion I pulled the toy to where the tip was almost completely out then slid as fast as I could till I was at the hilt with her. Her body shook with pleasure as her orgasim washed over both of us, once it tapered off we both fell to the bed in a heap of arms and legs. Looking down at my beautiful woman I began rubbing her arms lightly till she looked back at me, the toy still inside of her. Our lips touched and I saw her eyes had returned to their smoky blue color and with a sigh closed in a deep satisfied sleep. Slowly I pulled the toy out from between us with a sore pop. After I placed it on the bedside I clicked the light on the table off and relaxed back onto the pillows till my mind drifted off to the land of nod.

The scene in front of me was that of a back yard, I was in strange clothing as though it was in the 1930's. I had on a powder blue dress with white knee high socks. I looked to be about ten years old at this point and I was standing next to a blue and white beach ball, the sky had started clouding up again like it did last time my skin began prickling with anticipation as the hair on the back of my neck stood up. Looking around wildly I saw the same man from my last dream, he had on the same victorian outfit but was wearing a bowler hat this time with goggles on top. He was a good twenty yards away. As soon as I had blinked he was right in front of me where I was standing frozen to the spot. His hand shot out to my throat and touched the scar there where he had bitten me before. With a smile his garbled words scraped my ears.

"You're not quite done yet are you?" With a flash like a cobra he ripped out my throat once again where my blood sprayed out into the air. I felt myself being shaken awake out of my horrid nightmare, Tara was right above me with wild eyes switching back and forth between her natural blue to her angry gold.

"ZOEY! DAMNIT ZOEY WAKE UP!" with one last shake I gasped in my breath and looked up at her in a panic. "Zoey! Are you okay?!" her hand had started caressing my cheek.

"I'm fine just a nightmare is all, seriously I'm fine" I held her hand steady to my cheek "I just want to be held right now."

Tara immediately obliged by wrapping me into a warm hug and petting my hair telling me everything's okay. After what seemed like an hour I heard her light snoring as she had passed out again. Burying myself into her breasts I curled back and closed my eyes to return to sleep.

Chapter 13

Changes

Tara

It's been a week since my last change where I had wandered around in wolf form, every day that Jeremy hasn't had to work I have intruded on his time with every conceivable question that popped into my head. He says my progress has been wonderful and that the moon will only dictate full changes for the next few months, though full moons will be very difficult to ignore it is possible. It's taken him years to perfect that skill to control himself and that for the next full one he will show me a place in the rural areas of New York where we will be able to run free without hurting people.

Him and Tom go up there some weekends for alone time and rent a cabin during the off seasons so he can expend all of his extra energy out. Jeremy had told me that we could potentially make it a double date where Tom and Zoey can hang out and maybe work so neither one will be alone and bored out of their minds.

Zoey's nightmares have shaken me pretty hard and I always ask if she wants to talk about them but she has been mulishly silent on the subject. Either way I figure she will tell me when she is ready, I just need to be patient with her.

According to Jeremy the full moon will return every 28 days and lasts three nights though since I changed at the end of the cycle I may have to change on the first night. He did warn me that I will be a bit more aggressive and protective of what's mine, and the musky smell that always hangs around the room is called marking. Apparently wild animals do something similar with their mates so no other alpha or animal will go anywhere near them. He has taught me how to channel the wolf but has warned me several times to try not to use it around regular people because the way my eyes change could spook someone. When I asked why it was bad to spook people one day he laughed and explained it all to me.

"When people get scared they run, and when they run we have to chase. It's just primal instincts kicking in triggering that urge." Jeremy said "So unless you want to have the cops called on your ass for stalking I suggest that you avoid joggers and channeling your wolf especially during the week of the moon."

"What happens if I start changing in public? You said that I did well with my breathing exercises but what happens if my heart rate spikes or something happens where someone upsets me and I can't stop the change in time?" Curiosity was making me paranoid.

"Well… if that happens you better hope there is an alleyway or something close by where you can hide because if you can't calm yourself you may wake up in a ditch with blood all over you again and not realize that you killed someone till it's too late. Just try to stay calm." he gave me a sad knowing smile.

My biggest fear was killing someone again, from what the cleaning crew told Jeremy was the guy I had feasted on my first night had been arrested multiple times for robberies and abuse charges. He said at least I took the life of someone who the world could afford to lose, though it didn't make me relieved it's still better than attacking someone who had done nothing wrong before.

With a sigh I watched Tom picking up around the apartment and doing busy work as he waited for an email for his new project he was suppose to be working on with a hotel. Looking at Jeremy I smiled.

"So how do you rent one of those cabins? Do we go there or call ahead or something?" I questioned lightly.

"I have the number in my phone, but we can call with as little as a week in advance." smiling he pulled out his phone and went to the cabin's website. Turning the phone towards me he let me hold it to check out the pictures. The wooded areas looked beautiful and they had a lake! I could feel my eyes widen at the thought of going there soon.

"The cabin's are 2 bed 1 bath and have a fireplace in the living room with a full eat in kitchen so after a run with me we can and lay down next to the fire or return to our respective partners and cuddle up without things being awkward." he chuckled lightly as he rain his hand through his dirty blonde hair causing another thought to pop into my head.

"So… are you… like are you a blonde when you are a wolf? Or does that change too?"

"Well that all depends. My fur gets a little lighter till it's more of a normal blonde rather than this dirty blond that I have. Yours however went darker till it was almost fully black, as for your eyes, they turn a gold color while mine turn a brown color. That's the alpha coming through though. Alphas always have a brighter glowing eye color with dark fur, I don't know if it's a genetic thing coming through or just how our species functions to tell us who is in charge. Though from what I've see you and I are the only ones in the state of New York."

"Wait so I'm an Alpha? What does that make you?" I asked flabbergasted by his statement.

"Well while I had been alone for so long I was my own alpha, but since you are now here that knocked my rank right down to Beta, not a bad thing!" he exclaimed at my upset expression. "It just means that your dominate when it comes to hunting and such, I would follow your lead if we were to hunt as a pack."

From across the room I saw Tom chuckle at Jeremy as he walked to his laptop for the thousandth time to check his email once again. Jeremy's eyes turned to slits as he glowered at Tom's back.

"I also noticed...um, well when Zoey and I are... Intimate my wolf likes to sometimes... take control of me? I'm worried that it might hurt her..." I looked up at Jeremy with terror and concern.

"Well Zoey did speak to me about the first time that happened, Tom actually found a way to counteract that for me. I was the same way when I first started my first couple changes. All she has to do is use a commanding voice. The first time he did that to me I immediately ceased from my actions, confused the hell out of me the first few times actually but when he said to stop or to not do something it's like the wolf wants to listen to a stronger voice." with a shrug Jeremy looked at me with a smile.

Looking up at the clock I noticed that it was just a bit past 5pm already. "Shit Zoey's art show will be over soon, I gotta get back home and prepare. She keeps bringing Atlas with her when she goes. People seem to really enjoy his company and he helps to sell the art." I said with a grin as I stood up.

"Alright cousin, if you have any other questions or just wanna talk I am free this weekend for a few hours but I will set up our double for 3 weekends from now the full moon will be rising at exactly 8:30pm that night so we will go there the day before and just relax around the cabin so we can prepare ourselves, sound good?" I nodded in agreement as I walked to the door.

"Thank you again for all of what you have been doing, I know it can't be easy to talk about this kind of stuff with your cousin especially." I smiled sheepishly as I shut the door behind myself.

Walking down the stairs to my apartment I wandered in and raced to the bedroom, my excitement could be felt like lightning crackling through the air. Looking at myself in the mirror I stripped down to my underwear I grabbed a silk scarf from the bedside table and tied it right above my eyes. Sitting on the edge of the bed I pulled the blue dildo out from the table and placed it on the comforter. Putting earbuds in my ears I began playing music to where I couldn't hear the outside world, once that was finished I pulled my makeshift blindfold down over my eyes and laid down spreadeagled on the bed to wait patiently.

After about 10 minutes I smelled her sweet scent permeate the room, I bit my bottom lip in anticipation for our encounter and wiggled my hips suggestively. Cold hands wrapped around my ankles and pulled me to the baseboard where I felt fabric wrap around them both. Skilled fingers drifted up my legs and up my stomach till they stopped at my bra and circled just over the nipple. I felt a tugging on my wrists as they were then secured into place with the other scarve atop the headboard. I felt very exposed but also very excited as a hand trailed down my arm and cupped my chin to steal a kiss. The bed dipped at the base when a heavy weight settled onto the bottom and sat between my legs. A cold hand slid up my inner thigh as

Zoey's hand cupped my sex and began rubbing through my underwear with her palm. Without the help of vision or hearing it caused all of my other senses to go into overdrive, my nostrils began flaring as my skin burned at her touch. Her hand creeped downward to my slit and began stroking lightly through the fabric covering it, till I was squirming with anticipation.

I felt her hair on my leg as she bent down gently and kissed my thigh and trailed kisses up to my apex, her tongue snaked out and licked right above my underwear line as her teeth tore through the fabric in half. Her mouth was then on me taking my fold in her mouth and nibbling with her sharp teeth causing me to squirm like a fish on a hook. As her tongue found my internal cavern my hips rocketed off of the bed into her mouth, I could feel her rumble of laughter causing me to moan out in wanting.

Her cool body dragged up mine till I could feel her icy breath on my where she kissed my pulse point to where a small prick in my neck caused me to jolt a little before relaxing. Her hand trailed down my body to between my legs once again to play with my curls. As she fed from me her hand moved back up to my breasts I felt her body shift into position between my legs, a light pressure had started pushing into me. Once she had entered into me fully I felt her hand slowly make small circles along my clit till she sent me closer and closer to the edge. As the music in my ears crescendoed I couldn't hold myself back any further and tugged as hard as possible on my bonds as I lept from the edge into orgasim.

Once the fog lifted from my vision I felt hands behind my head untying my blindfold, blinking up at her our lips met in a sweet slow kiss. As she untied my hands I removed the earbuds while she worked to undo my feet.

"How did the art show go?" I smiled at her beautiful naked ass presented to me as she bent over.

"It went well I sold 3 paintings today and got Atlas a toy for being so good." she looked back at me with a smile. The dildo was still hanging between her legs that swayed as she moved to my other foot to undo it. Reaching between her legs I gently tugged on it successfully freezing her into place.

"I thought you promised me that I could use this on you if I was a good girl?" I tugged lightly again causing her to moan loudly.

"I did say that didn't I." Zoey's voice had become breathy. Slowly I pulled till the holding part had popped out of her sending shivers up her spine.

"Watch me now." When she turned her head to me I laid back and inserted the part I had just removed from her into myself all while never breaking eye contact. Her mouth dropped open slightly as her eyes became hooded, just as she was about ready to turn I sat up and grabbed her hips stilling her from moving. "Oh no you don't." I said with a chuckle "I told you it was my turn to do this to you."

Getting into position behind her I pushed her front down till her face was pressed into the mattress. Using the end of the toy I circled her opening gently till she whimpered for me to use it on her properly. Slowly I slipped the tip into her opening and assumed a position over her till our shoulders touched and my breasts were firmly against her back. I could feel the wolf trying to take control as I felt my legs start to shake. Taking a deep breath I relinquished a bit of control and felt my mind get shoved back. I felt like I was watching a porno movie as I saw myself start humping Zoey wildly as I slammed into her. Our body's mingling till we were both panting for breath and sweating heavily, our skin sticking together with sweat and love juices. I felt my legs move to where I was practically sitting on top of her while pounding away.

Guttural noises were coming out from between my lips as my body picked up speed, I heard a snarl rip through the quiet room as we saturated the toy with our slick juices. My hips were like a machine that kept ramming into her as she started to cry out in pleasure, I felt my mouth pin the back of her neck down as I bit her while we fucked. Zoey cried out loudly as she tipped over the edge with a large shiver, my hips slowly started to slow down and I smelled a thick musky odor in the room again as the wolf finished with her. Slowly I gained control back as it faded out to where I gently removed the toy from both of us as we fell back onto the bed in a sweaty heap on the covers.

Chapter 14

Escapades

Tara

The week of the full moon my skin felt as though it was on fire, every time that I moved my arms would tense up as though the muscles were spasming from unused energy. Every so often I would keep either checking my phone or the calendar before pacing around the apartment for the umpteenth time. Zoey had gone to another one of her art showings earlier that morning that would be lasting for three full days up the street. I did ask if I could come with her this time just to get out of the house but Jeremy, Tom, and herself all told me the same thing.

"During this time you really shouldn't go outside till we get to the cabin, it could be too dangerous if you happen to wander off and get caught up by the smells of the city."

Well tell that to my skin! Scratching at my shoulder again I made another lap around the living and kitchen area, and with an exasperated sigh sat down on the couch trying to relax. Turning the tv on I channel hopped before settling on the cooking station, they had a contest going on where everyone was cooking out on grills in the pouring rain.

Snorting with annoyance I looked out the window. *Of course it's a beautiful sunny day outside, it can't be crappy and nasty out… maybe I could just go for a jog, wear some earbuds to block out the sounds and put vapo rub under my nose?* The idea wasn't half bad, getting up I wandered to the bedroom and found a pair of workout pants with a tight t-shirt and hoodie. Grabbing my Ipod off the bedside I walked into the bathroom and looked in the medicine cabinet for the nasty smelling jelly.

After I got myself situated I grabbed the set of keys Zoey had given me and threw on a pair of running shoes we had bought for me a week ago. Jeremy had said it was a good idea to get a pair cause I would run right out of my normal shoes if I had the chance to really get going. Walking out the door I checked my pockets for everything, I was missing my phone but I was only going for a quick jog not a trans continental journey. Locking the door behind myself I quickly sprinted down the stairs and put the earbuds in each ear, the vapo rub was doing its job very well no city smell was catching my attention and the music pounding in my ears was successfully blocking out any noises that would cause me to lose my focus.

Within seconds my feet were moving like a well oiled machine, each step sending a pleasurable jolt up my legs till I was running. The sky was a beautiful perfect blue as the sunlight reflected off of the skyscraper windows, my breathing started to match my sprints as I made it 5 blocks within two minutes.

My little jog lasted till I made it a total of about a full two miles before looking around at my surroundings again and realizing that I was back at the park where I had apparently had my little episode. My eyes darted around the park as I saw a baseball game in full swing, walking down the concrete path I noticed a stain under a street light that was quite large and looked as though someone had tried to scrub it out. Blinking lightly a flash of memory flew through my brain.

I followed the scent closely with my nose pressed upon the earth till a popping noise crossed my path. Looking up I saw a man standing over a body with a gun. I felt a deep rumbling growl bubble up from my chest, the smell of blood was driving me crazy. The man looked up and saw me, terror flashed across his face as he raised the gun to point it towards me.

I lept at him as another series of pops echoed across the park, a burning sensation skimmed my right shoulder as I tackled him to the ground and ripped his throat out. His body began convulsing in on itself as my claws dug deep into his exposed skin. The last thought I had before I blacked out was how delicious it all was.

Retching in the nearby trash can I couldn't hold my stomach back, my brain kept throwing images of the expression on his face as I tore his flesh from his bones.

It took a good five minutes to calm myself down a bit before I was able to get up and sprint back to the apartment I barely checked my speed, to passersby I must have looked as though I was running from someone. My nose burned as the vapo rub smell had started to fade and the smell of the city began enticing me with its enchanting aroma.

Shaking my head hard I started running faster till I reached the sandstone building, I couldn't get my keys out fast enough. Once I opened the door I looked up and saw Zoey standing in the middle of the living room with her jaw set in displeasure and her arms crossed over her chest.

"So. you decided to take matters into your own hands about the whole changing thing didn't you…" her voice was frigid towards me with a commanding stance.

"I just… I had to go for a run, I felt trapped in here…" I looked down from her as her foot started tapping.

"Do you know just how worried I was? You didn't answer! I thought someone might have taken you again!" With a sigh she shook her head and threw her hands up in the air as she walked to the bedroom and closed the door lightly. Atlas looked up at me from the floor and snorted as he walked to his bed in the corner.

Nice to have someone on my side I glared after the dog.

Wandering over to the couch I sat down and pulled my knees up to my chest with a sigh, the itching burning of my skin continued till my spine started to tingle. I started pacing the room again trying to get rid of the annoying sensation. My hands kept rubbing the muscles in my arms as my back spasmed and twitched every couple of seconds. The bedroom door opened to reveal Zoey in a leather thong and breasts tied up in leather cords, her silk teal colored robe falling open to reveal thigh high boots and a leather leash on her hip.

"So you wanna disobey me when I gave you a direct order?" her voice had turned dominate.

"I didn't mean to worry you I'm sorry." I pleaded with her

"Did I say you could fucking talk?" her voice rose a few octaves "get on all fours and you better be naked when I come back." as she walked into the bedroom I stripped as fast as possible. Hoping to please her, I could feel my eyes change as my skin burned hot as an oven.

Assuming the position she told me to be in I sat eagerly on the balls of my feet and waited for her to get back. Within three or four minutes she returned and walked over to me, as she bent down close to me I felt her hands go around my neck as she hooked a collar up to me. When she stood she had the leash in one hand and a small leather whip. My nostrils flared out at the sight of the crevice between her legs, I couldn't resist.

She wants to play this game? I'll play this game. With a lurch I rammed my face into her crotch and began licking eagerly at her folds through the thongs fabric, while she tried to keep her balance from my attack. A strong tug pulled me backwards as she removed me from her wetness.

"Oh no you don't, today it's my turn to be in control of you."

Her voice turned singsong as she led me back to the bedroom and tied the leash onto the bed giving me maybe three feet of leeway to move around. "You are gonna stay there till I get a proper apology. And you are not permitted to use your hands at all, if you use them on me or yourself I will whip you like the dog you are." she grinned at the thought. "And I won't be gentle, otherwise how will you learn?"

My excitement was building at the prospect of being whipped by her as I moved till I was on the floor between her legs. They were closed tight in front of me, remembering what she had said about using my hands I quickly nudged her knees with my nose till I made it halfway between her legs. Letting the wolf in me make a few noises, I whimpered as she tried closing around my head.

"What is it girl? You wanna play?" Zoey teased "do you need me to do something?" she grinned maliciously.

"I need you to-" the spike of the whip flashed up my spine causing me to yelp. Looking into her eyes I frowned.

"I still didn't say you could fucking talk now did I?" she grinned showing off her fangs. Instead of answering I just shook my head keeping my mouth shut. "Thats a good girl." her legs parted enough to allow my head access to her sweet spot.

Diving between her legs I pressed my nose close to her crotch in hopes of getting into her faster. As I lunged the leash tugged hard against my neck stopping me before I could really get to work. Looking back at where she had tied me I glowered at the bedpost then at her face where she had an innocent expression plastered.

"Need some help?" Laughter was evident in her voice as she teased me. When I stayed mute her eyes glowed as a slow smile spread along her lips. "I guess not. Oh well." She scooted back till she was laying seductively on the bed, her hand trailed down her body as she slowly removed the thong and threw it across the room revealing her sweet spot that I wanted to dive into so badly. "Too bad, I was hoping to get some puppy love today." her peal of laughter sent shivers through me as she slowly began pleasuring herself without my help. Letting my control falter I felt my eyes turn the bright golden yellow as the wolf began to make a whimpering growl noise.

"What's wrong girl? Were you expecting to get off the hook that easily?" I shifted on my hips as my thighs began rubbing together trying to quell the ache that had formed between my own legs. I whimpered again as she started to slip her fingers in and out of herself. "Oh no, due to your... insubordination you are gonna sit there like a good dog and watch me get myself off. No touching, no talking, and definitely no pleasing yourself. Got it?" my brow creased at her words, she didn't want to make love, she wanted to punish me for my little escapade I had taken around the city.

"Zoey please-" my voice had begun warping. Her eyes had trapped me in a trance, stopping me from continuing the sentence.

"Tara, you really don't want to finish that sentence." as her head laid back I sat in silence and watched as she continued to please herself. Her hand picked up speed as her body began arcing causing her to moan and buck. For what seemed like an eternity I stared as she pleasured herself without my help and wanted so badly to join her. With a sigh I turned away and leaned against the bed as she finished, her moans echoed around the room as she climaxed.

When her breathing slowed down I peeked behind myself only to be greeted by her face just inches from my own. I felt an acrid uncomfortable sensation bubble up from my stomach that burned my throat and caused my face to flush unhappily. Looking away from her I felt her hands slowly touch my shoulders and slowly move downward till she had cupped my breasts. I ignored the sensation of pleasure that had started and focused on the wall till her mouth came to my neck. My anger had built to an alarming level in the short time of me sitting at the foot of the bed.

"Tara?" her voice was husky in my ear. "Come to me sweetheart."

"Am I permitted to talk?" my voice sounded wrong in my ears, my displeasure was very evident. "Or must I be tortured again with your teasing and rejection?" I felt her body tense up at my tone, her hand moved up to the collar around my neck as she unlatched the hook on the ring. Her arms wrapped around me in a hug as she held onto me tightly.

"I'm... I'm sorry Tara, I don't know what to say." her hand moved to my cheek to turn my head to try and kiss me.

"No." I felt defiant, my voice had started warping again and my mouth felt as though I had too many teeth, the wolf was not pleased that she had been denied pleasure. Zoey's body froze solid as she gazed at me, she almost resembled a statue.

I quickly got up from my position and began pacing like a caged animal, my skin was on fire as the hair on my arms began prickling with electricity once again. Every so often I would look at her as she sat on the edge of the bed with a worried expression growing evident on her face. I didn't care at this point, I just kept pacing. When she went to get off the bed I felt a deep throaty growl bubble up from my chest causing her to cease all movement.

I stopped at the window and looked out at the city, the sky was a beautiful midnight blue as the almost full moon peaked through the clouds. My hair had started raising up in anticipation as I resumed my pacing once again, my muscles burned hotly at the prospect of a chase I felt my legs twitching with every step. Zoey hadn't moved again from her position on the bed except to watch me pace. My hands kept rubbing at the muscles that would occasionally spasm to where I would stop to look out the window once again. With a sigh I leaned against the glass and stared out at the city without seeing anything except for the moon.

Zoey gently padded over to me and stood a few feet back, not touching me. The smell of my musk permeated the air, I saw her tantalizing reflection in the glass as she held herself lightly. I saw her step foward a few steps till she was directly behind me as she dropped to her knees. Frowning I looked behind myself at where she sat, her head was bowed exposing the back of her neck and her hands were bracing her torso up off the floor, she was presenting herself to me. My hair bristled on end at the beautiful display causing me to turn and face her, her eyes never leaving the floor. A familiar wetness began pooling between my legs as I watched her sit, the wolf in me was pleased from her submission to where I released the rest of my control. I needed this badly, **I am the Alpha**.

My vision fogged up till I wasn't in control of my own body anymore, I could see a blurry screen of the room with Zoey being the center of attention. The colors of everything faded till all that stuck out were bright reds, yellows, and blues. The wolf was in full control.

With a shiver I felt my body move to right in front of her, my hands grabbed her hair to pull her head up till her eyes met mine, the beautiful glowing purple seemed to x-ray me. They widened as she looked up with curious anticipation, my lips parted revealing the much more pointed teeth that had grown in. Spreading my legs in front of me I looked down at her with wild eyes.

"You are going to get me off now, you may use what you need to to do so but you may not pleasure yourself. Understood?" she nodded quickly. I released her head as she crawled up between my legs and looked up at me with her wide eyes, her tongue licked her lip as her eyes trailed down to my labia. When her lips parted showing her fangs I added. "And you may not feed from me this time." her eyes shot up to meet my frosty stare, her skin had paled to the color of paper as she bit her bottom lip. When she nodded I leaned against the wall and opened my legs up to her.

She crawled over to where I was standing and slowly stretched herself up till she was face to face with my genitals. Quick as a flash she had her mouth on me, sucking at the opening and digging deeper into my cavern with her tongue. A longing moan escaped my lips as I let my head fall back to the wall, my hands started to trace down to her silky hair that had cascaded over her shoulders in beautiful mahogany waves. Holding onto her head I pressed her deeper into my slit till she had to adjust her position to get comfortable. I felt the pleasure building as my legs began shaking harder and harder while she licked and sucked at the folds. Tugging her hair lightly I pulled her head back and looked down at her.

"Lay on the ground face up." As her expression darkened in confusion I glared. "I intend to sit on your face." I gave her a wolfish grin. When she nodded I released her hair as she laid on the rug in the center of the room.

Wandering over to her lazily I circled her a few times till she was situated. When she finally stilled herself I got on my knees at the top of her head and slowly sat in position till I had a perfect view of her breasts and legs. Sinking down slowly I stopped when I felt her mouth attached to me once again as my body arched up in pleasure.

"That's a good girl." my hands cupped her breasts and I was rewarded with a gasp as my fingers flicked her nipples lightly sending a thrill through me. Slowly I bent down till my nose was pressed into her belly and I began nibbling the skin around her navel causing her to squirm and moan in pleasure. Making my way further down south I saw that her clitoris had engorged itself with need, my tongue started hanging out of my mouth as I panted heavily like a dog. Rubbing my nose into her I gave a long slow lick to her entire genital region leaving them slick with want. Her needy moan sent a reverberation through my own crevice as I did it again and again. I felt my hips working up and down as I began to hump her face, I slid two fingers into her sweet spot and started moving my hand with the tempo of my hips.

Our bodies started to saturate each other as we both became covered in sweat once again, both of us moaning in wild pleasure and both wanting more of each other. Suddenly I stopped and shot off of her body, looking down at her she had tangles in her hair and her mouth was soaked from me. With a devilish grin I laid on top of her in missionary style and lifted her knee till it was between my legs and mine between hers. Slowly I circled my hips till we had found a pattern of pleasure, her hand reached up to my breasts and began rubbing my nipples and bringing her face up till she suckled lightly on it.

My hand trailed down her body till I could feel her sweat slick heat flowing into my hand, I once again slipped two fingers in and began moving my hips faster shoving my hand in deeper inside her while building my own pleasure till we both cried out at our climax. I felt my voice crescendo towards the sky in an almost wolf like howl. The sound reverberated off of the walls as we finished each other off and slowed down to a lazy pace. Both of our breathing had become heavily labored as I collapsed in a heap on top of her, I slowly removed my fingers from her and sighed in pleasure.

R.J. Young

"I'm sorry I scared you." my voice had started turning back to normal I kissed the top of her head with my apology.

"I'm sorry I denied you pleasure… I might not understand how powerful the urges you have are but I am willing to learn… I'm sorry." Zoey hugged me closely. "If you need to go for a run again, could you please take your phone with you just so I don't worry?" her request was simple but I knew it would give her a piece of mind as we learned to trust each other more and slowly I nodded in agreement.

Chapter 15

The Cabin

My excitement had built to an exciting level as we left the city limits behind, the full moon was tomorrow and we were on the road in Tom's SUV. Zoey and I had put Atlas in a puppy daycare while were away, figuring that it would be safer for him away from wolves till I could get better control of myself. Though we were currently sharing the backseat and were cuddled up to each other occasionally kissing the others neck or letting a hand trail down between one's legs and circling around gently. Always when Jeremy and Tom were busy talking amongst themselves, it had turned into almost a game of how low can we go without being caught. Zoey's hand had slipped down my back and was right in the waistband of my underwear as we putted on down the road.

I grabbed the blanket we had tossed in the back and covered our legs up so we wouldn't look strange sitting so damn close to one another. As soon as I brought the blanket under my chin and over my shoulder her hand was on my back again in a flash unhooking my bra as she spoke freely with the guys. I felt my face heat up as her hand went down south to the button on my jeans and expertly unhooked them. I slowly closed my eyes and feigned sleep as she trailed her hand into the curls down below. My excitement evident in my panties as she felt the wetness I knew was there. Her fingers were like a butterfly fluttering over the hair till they landed in the sweet nectar residing there.

Her hand froze in place till I looked up at her shocked expression and smiled my wolfish grin. Her smile matched my own as her fingers resumed exploring below as she gently petted my ringlets and let her fingers dance in my free flowing juices. I had to hold back quite a few moans as she circled around my clitoral area, when she made it to my labia I bit my lip hard to stop any sound from escaping while still trying to feign sleep. The road had turned bumpy as we made it further out into the cabins territory Zoey shoved her fingers at my entrance as we hit certain bumps they would drive themselves deeper into me causing me to squirm excitedly.

Her fingers suddenly left me and she had buttoned up my pants faster than my eyes could see while hooking my bra back in place. Blinking I looked up at her with a sexually frustrated frown she had an expression of sincere amusement as she looked out the window at the forest surrounding the car, just through a manmade path was a beautiful little log cabin tucked away in the clearing that you would have missed it unless you knew where you were.

Tossing the blanket off myself I couldn't get out of the car fast enough, my nostrils flared out wide taking in the fresh smells and sights. My ears perked up as I heard the noise of birds chirping and animals running around, looking at Jeremy he had on a goofy grin as he also took in everything. Zoey tossed a bag at me to get my attention and I looked and saw our luggage being unloaded waiting to be taken inside. With a pout I grabbed some of the bags and dragged them to the open door and stepped in.

The walls were covered in a beautiful oak wood while the kitchen and living room shared the same deep color the floors were a bright cheerful honey color, Going to the opposite room of the guys a bathroom separated them, nothing too fancy about it, they had a double shower with seating area with a toilet and vanity. The walls were a cheerful blue color with seashell trim around the crown molding. Looking around our bedroom there was a giant king size taking up most of the room with matching bedside tables and pillows everywhere, the walls were the same wood that was in the main area as the wooden floors carried in.

Zoey came up and hugged me from behind and grabbed my breasts. "Looks like we need to break in the bed. What do you think dear?" I turned around quickly and enveloped her in a deep moaning kiss. Our breathing picked up quickly as I reached around her and shut the door, our bodies intertwining as we desperately tried to strip as fast as possible. Looking down I fiddled with the button of her jeans as my other hand explored between her legs, something was wrong there. Breaking our kiss apart I looked between us as I peeked in her underwear I saw the dark blue dildo poking out of the top of her jeans. My mouth dropped open in shock and awe as I looked at her.

"Well I couldn't think of where to put it to surprise you so I figured I would wear it. The past two hours have been torture on me just so you know." she grinned at my expression. "Come on, you ride on top." as she led us to the bed she stripped the rest of her clothes off and laid face up so the penis was standing at full attention. I eagerly took my pants off and clambered on top of her, as I went to pull my shirt off her hands stilled mine. "Leave it on, I think nothing is more sexy than a half dressed well fucked woman." Her eyes glinted in the muted light gleefully. Her hand reached up and undid my hair tie till all of my dark brown waves flowed down past my shoulders.

Still on my knees I scooted into position till I was poised and ready for her to enter me, her hands traced along my bare ass as her nails dug into my pale skin. I slowly slid a hand down myself and put two fingers at my own entrance while my other hand grasped the toy firmly and gave an experimental tug causing her to gasp in pleasure. Looking deep into her eyes I parted my lips down below and began sliding it into myself, moaning in pleasure. My hands shot out to each side of her head as her hips began working up and down into me matching my pace, I buried my face into the pillow to expose my neck as she sank her fangs into me.

A deep growl began building in my belly as she entered me from two points. Our bare hips smacking together in fiery passion, she unhooked my bra and helped me get it off while keeping my shirt on, as she pulled my head down for a kiss her finger began sliding between us till she made it to my clit. Her frozen hands burned my heated skin till all

I could do was cry out in pleasure as we climaxed together. When we finished I fell back onto the bed and just stared at her in awe.

"I love you Zoey" we both froze with realization as my statement hung in the air. Looking deeply in each others eyes I felt a burning desire to feed and pleasure her.

"I love you too Tara" our lips met together and we continued to round two.

Chapter 16

Romping

After we all settled into our respective rooms we had all joined up into the living room, Tom had brought in firewood and had built roaring flames. Jeremy looked at me and gestured to follow him outside. When we excused ourselves we began walking along the path to where the forest had started forming.

"I want to do a little exercise with you." Jeremy looked down at me when we made it to a clearing. "Breath in deeply and start releasing the control you have. Not too much just yet but enough to where your senses become heightened." with a nod I did as he asked and felt my skin tingle as the wolf started to awaken. Looking up at him I saw his blue eyes had turned a deep woodsy brown and his mouth had puffed out a little bit. My nostrils flared as his scent hit me, it was a low burning smell that raised the hair on my neck up and warned me of danger, a deep growl bubbled through my lips causing my eyes to widen.

"I'm sorry!" I smacked my hand over my mouth to stop from doing it again. With a chuckle Jeremy removed my hand from my mouth and gave me a small smile.

"You're doing just fine." his smell was right under my nose with his hand so close, the smell caused my hair to stand on edge again as my eyes narrowed dangerously making my lip twitch up to reveal my teeth. His eyes dropped from mine as he removed his hand, he seemed to be in a confused pain as though he couldn't look me in the eyes. "It's just our wolves meeting for-" his lips started twitching slightly as he bared his teeth "t-the first time. They have to g-get to know each other so we know not to kill one another when we go h-hunting." his head began bowing till he had dropped lower than my eyes and exposed the back of his neck.

Air snorted out of my nose as I took in his scent, my control slipped further as I began circling around him, all colors started draining from the world except for his red shirt and the yellow from the trees. My mind was shoved to the back of my head as I dropped on all fours, I had no more control of my body as I circled him tighter. Jeremy had laid fully on the ground exposing his chest and stomach to me, his teeth still bared in submission to my dominance. I felt myself getting drawn closer to him as my mouth opened and my lips twitched in displeasure. I could almost physically see his wolf crouched in terror as my reflection shown in his eyes. Before I could stop myself my mouth had lashed out and grabbed him around the neck, biting down as he thrashed and yelped under me.

His cries echoed around the forest till I heard two people running, my eyes locked on to Zoey and Thomas standing frozen in the thicket at the sight before them. My fangs in Jeremy's neck with him not trying to move and a deep growl building in the electrified air. *I could snap his windpipe and he would never challenge me again.* The thought raced through my head as my musky smell permeated the air, my hands had turned to claws digging into his shirt as I stared our partners down. When Tom went to take a step forward I dug my teeth in deeper till Jeremy let another yelp out.

His voice came out in a raspy whisper. "I'm fine Tommy her Alpha is just-" I growled deeper silencing him. His whole body began shaking and finally went limp going fully submissive to me. With what seemed like two or three breaths that could have been an eternity, my wolf finally released him as I backed up. I stared him down till he rolled over and refused to look me directly in the eye. His neck had pinprick marks where my teeth had been, I could see the bruises forming already from how hard I bit him. I snorted at his weakness and felt a howl building in my throat as I released it he joined me. In one fluid motion my wolf relaxed back to where I regained full control once again. Rushing over to Jeremy I hugged him tight.

"I am so so sorry! I don't know what came over me! Oh god you're bleeding!" I touched his neck lightly as both of our eyes changed back to their normal blue color. Thomas ran over to us with Zoey close behind.

"Maybe you both shouldn't change together?" Tom's voice was shaking with anger. "I would rather have a husband that is fully intact if you don't mind." his eyes met mine and I felt the heat of his stare.

"Tommy it's not her fault. She was just doing what I told her to do." Jeremy sat up angrily "Now that our wolves have met there won't be a bloodbath when we meet in wolf form."

"I DON'T CARE ABOUT THAT JEREMY! She could have KILLED you!" his voice had gotten progressively louder as his anger bubbled over, I had never seen Tom lose control like that.

"Tom. Leave it." Jeremy got up and walked back towards the cabin as Tom jumped up and followed after him, still bickering about what had happened.

I didn't realize I was crying till my tears started spilling down onto my hands. Zoey was right next to me hugging me close in hopes of calming me down.

"Don't worry love. Jeremy knew what he was doing, it's all just really new to us." Standing up she pulled my arm till I was leaning on her. "Come on, Tom will calm down, no worries."

Walking back to the cabin with Zoey I heard silence when we got to the door. As we walked in Tom looked up from the couch where he had hooked up his computer and gave me a sad smile. Putting his laptop down he wandered over to me and pulled me into a giant bear hug.

"I'm sorry for yelling sweet pea, just seeing Jeremy like that really scared the bejeezus out of me. I've never seen him in that situation before. I'm sorry." When I hugged him back Zoey shot me an I told you so look with a giant smile.

"I don't know what came over me. I would never do that to him normally but my wolf is just… she's just so strong…" my voice quavered at the end.

"It ain't your fault love, just relax. Jeremy says since you guys met in human form with the wolves in control you shouldn't wanna kill each other when in wolf form." Stepping back from me he smiled. "Let's get some good food going and fill our bellies." when he wandered to the kitchen Zoey kissed my neck and smiled.

After a good solid meal and a long car trip my body was ready to sleep the day away. Zoey and I made it to our bedroom and within minutes both of us were down for the count. It wasn't till the midday sun peeked through the curtains that I stirred from my slumber, with a long stretched out yawn I cracked my back and looked over at the clock.

IT'S ALREADY THREE!? With a jolt of panic I jumped up from the bed and scrambled around for clean clothes. Just as I opened the door Jeremy was standing in the doorway blocking my exit.

"Well good morning to you too." He said with a chuckle. "Are you ready to go? I figured we could hike around for a little bit till we had to come home and prepare for this evening. It would give us a better lay of the land while we are out galavanting around."

"That sounds… fun." I said with a sleepy yawn.

"Well it's either check out the sites or wait another 6 hours for the regulars to arise from their slumber." he grinned playfully at me.

"Well as long as we can see the lake they have in the pictures I will be happy." I grinned back at him.

The walk around the trails was fairly enjoyable, Jeremy shared his stories with me about his first time coming to this place before he met Tom. It took him forever to even trust someone with his secret before he revealed it to him. By the time we had seen the beautiful scenic view and made it back to the cabin the clock on the wall proclaimed the time to be 7:45 pm. Zoey and Tom had gotten up they said an hour ago but from the look of the fresh coffee in hand I highly doubted their story. When 8pm rolled around Jeremy gave Tom a kiss and nuzzled his neck, I noticed his eyes had turned the deep brown again.

I felt the hair on my arms standing on edge anytime I moved, my eyes would spiral in and out from blue to gold just depending on what I was doing, it had an almost dizzying effect on my brain. Every sight, every smell, even every little noise would catch my attention and the wolf would be ready to do something. Kissing Zoey I whispered that I loved her and would be back a little later.

The sensations tripled as I walked outside in the cool breeze, the air burned my lungs as the night expanded outward, I saw a sliver of the moon through the trees. Jeremy had started walking behind the cabin to the open shower stall to start his change, he explained to me that we should keep our clothes somewhere easily found just so we don't wind up losing them. Taking the other side of the stall I began stripping down and just stood in the nude, unsure of what to do.

"Uh... Jeremy?" I felt exposed and foolish for not knowing. A deep dog like growl answered me, I saw that he was on all fours and his skin was bubbling maliciously as new fur sprouted all over him. Copying his position I took a deep breath and relinquished my hold on the wolf once more.

My body began to violently shaking it felt as though my skin was eating me from the inside out. My eyes rolled into the back of my head and I was twitching violently.

I felt the hair on my arms growing my skin had grown super sensitive as more deep brown almost black hair sprouted all over my body. My face felt like it was stretching as every bone in my body snapped and regrew longer. Falling to the ground fully I saw my fingers shrinking before being overtaken by more hair. My arms and legs turned more dog like as a strange sensation prickled my tailbone, my neck elongated till I blacked out.

When I awoke I heard a whimpering from over top of me, a light brown wolf was pawing at the ground in a playful manner, I felt gangly and stiff as I raised up. Examining myself I looked up at the other wolf in confusion and looked behind myself. There was something there moving.

I HAVE A TAIL! Looking at the other wolf I stepped out of the stall and took in the sights and smells. Breathing in the odors one in particular caught my attention causing me to race around the side of the cabin with Jeremy at my heels. Stopping under the window I sat up till my hind legs were holding me up the windowsill. I was able to peek into Zoey and my bedroom and had a perfect view of my lovely partner spread out on the bed in nothing but her mandala robe, one arm under her head as her other hand was between her legs. She was staring at the ceiling in boredom gently playing with herself. I whimpered lightly at the sight in front of me and pawed at the window catching her attention. She quickly removed her hand and scrambled off the bed closing her robe up. When I barked at the window and pawed playfully she frowned and walked over to open it. For the first time I met her face to face in this form without an ounce of fear between us. I sniffed her hand she had on the windowsill and licked off the juices that were there with a whimper.

"Tara?" my head lolled into her as I began sniffing in the V of her robe giving her little love bites and licking her exposed skin. When I made it to her breasts she froze and stepped back looking at me with her eyebrow up. "Oh no you don't. I'm not into that whole... human animal thing. So take that bright idea and go jump in the lake with it." when I let out a pitiful whine she tilted her head to the side in exasperation "No, I'm not saying no to you, I'm saying no to you in this form. Argue with me all you want but I ain't budging on this. Now shoo go play" she began whisping her hands at me to get me off the sill. When I dropped back down to all fours she shut and locked the window with a grin and went back to bed.

Looking behind myself Jeremy had been looking pointedly away from me and gave me a sideways glance before wandering to his and Tom's window. Looking right at me he lifted his leg as though to mark his territory. My alpha didn't like that at all and caused me to sprint directly towards him and tackle his ass to the ground in a growling barking heap. I heard Zoey open the window as Tom came running out the front door. Jeremy and I were biting and scratching at each other so loudly you would think we were trying to kill ourselves.

I successfully pinned him down again but instead of relenting he kept squirming till I gave an alpha growl, the audience watched as he slowed his struggle. When his tail went between his legs I smell the acrid scent of piss. I released him and looked up at Zoey in defiance at her telling me no. Almost in a look what I would do for you show.

With a solid bark I nudged Jeremy upward and began trotting along the trail, my tail was straight up and every wag of it sprayed my musky odor all over the path I took. Jeremy was following next to me but never getting ahead, sniffing every so often for the smell of some prey. After a few minutes he stopped dead and nudged my flank and made a sniffing the air motion. My nostrils flared for the smell and I caught a tantalizing odor of a large animal, following the smell we set off till we were downwind of a doe. She had her head bent down and was chewing on a patch of grass at her hooves.

Creeping on our bellies Jeremy scuttled over to her right while I flanked her left till we were just a few yards away, the leaves on the ground were wet under my feet from rain a few days ago and muffled all sounds I made. The doe raised her head up and looked to her right where Jeremy lept from his hiding spot and went for a flying tackle grabbing her neck. As he charged I ran and slid under her and began clawing on my back at her belly as her hooves bucked and squirmed, her insides came spilling on top of me covering my fur with blood and organ tissue. With a final crunch Jeremy had snapped her neck and the doe fell to the ground dead.

Wiggling myself out from under the corpse I looked over at Jeremy who was also covered in the deer's blood. Gently I padded over to him and began grooming his fur while he did the same to mine. Looking down at our prize I grabbed the things leg and began making a tugging motion for him to do the same. With each of us having a leg in our mouth we dragged our trophy back towards the cabin. When we made it to the clearing at the front door I dropped the beast's leg and walked to the door. Sending a loud howl out of my throat.

The reaction was almost comical, I heard plates crash inside as heavy foot falls raced to open the door. As it swung open I saw Tom standing with the light from the living room behind him looking down with utter terror at me covered in blood. When Jeremy padded up behind me his stance relaxed noticeably.

"Zoey! You have a delivery!" Tom grinned at me as my tongue lolled out of my mouth, my tail wagged back and forth in excitement.

"Tom, what are you- OH MY GOD!" Zoey saw all the blood that had been splattered over both Jeremy and myself, her eyes immediately changed to their deep purple color. "What the Fuck Tara!?" She looked past us and saw the mangled body of the deer in the light of the porch. Her lips hardened to a thin line as she blinked a few times. My tail had stopped wagging as I watched her expression with bated breath, my tongue had returned back into my mouth. I sat down like a good girl and gave her puppy dog eyes while my ears pressed down to the top of my head.

After a few heartbeats Tom nudged her hip with his own. "Say thank you Zoey." Zoey looked over at him in shock and annoyance.

"She's providing food for you, it's basically a gift…" Tom was still trying to hold in his laughter. My head dipped downward to peek up at her waiting to either be reprimanded or thanked.

With a sigh Zoey gave me an endearing smile and patted my head gently. "Thank you my dear but I am fine right-" before she could finish I tackled her to the ground and pinned her down with kisses along her neck and cheeks, trying to get as close to her as possible. My tail was like a helicopter as I cuddled up to her and laid down on her chest with a stupid doggy grin.

"EW! God you smell like ass!" Zoey's nose scrunched up in displeasure as she caught my scent. "You badly need a bath!" hopping up off of her I circled around her and nipped her butt when she got up causing her to let off a squeal. "No! Go, go to the bathroom right this minute young lady." she pointed in the direction of the shower.

Bounding past everyone I slid over the hardwood floors leaving bloody paw prints and skid marks all over the wooden floors. I sat on the rug in the bathroom and waited patiently for her to join me, my tail never stopped wagging with excitement. Zoey passed by the bathroom and went into our room confusing me. I followed her into our room and watched as she took her robe off and dug in her suitcase for something. Her scent had permeated the air in the room where she had pleasured herself earlier leaving me wanting her. I bowed my head to the floor and began sniffing around the bed till I found where she had finished herself. My nose pressed into the sheets leaving blood smears all over the down comforter. Licking at the spot on the bed I was able to taste her pleasure while sending shivers up my back and flanks. Looking at her bent over I padded quietly over to her rear and shoved my nose into her crease.

She yelped loudly and nearly jumped out of her skin as she fell to the ground. Glaring up at me I tilted my head and let my tongue loll out of my mouth causing her to laugh and push me off of herself.

"I already told you I'm not into that kind of stuff." she patted my head lightly. "I know it's still you in there but the way you look now in this form is giving me a lot of concerns." shaking her head she grabbed her bathing suite she was trying to wrangle out of the suitcase and slipped it on effectively hiding her body from my prying wolfy eyes, when my ears fell she frowned.

"Don't be giving me that look, I'm not happy about this situation anymore than you are. Come on, let's get you all cleaned up." As she walked to the bathroom I padded after her with my head low, grumbling every few seconds at her, when I sat down on the rug she turned the shower on full blast and closed the door behind us. I immediately eyeballed the closed door as she prepared the water for me. Looking at her balefully I ignored her calls at trying to get me into the steamy water and stuck my nose up at her when she called my name.

"Damnit Tara get in the damn shower." when I huffed at her she came up behind me and grabbed my torso to try to pick me up. I made myself into dead weight and rolled on my back as refusal for her efforts.

"Fuck it!" her bathing suite was covered in blood from my fur ruining the powder blue design on it. Reaching behind herself she undid her top and bottoms and let them fall to the ground, tossing them to the shower's floor she stepped in after them and sat on one of the two ledges there. And began scrubbing the fabric with soap trying to get the stains off. Hopping up I stepped into the shower and squished myself against her body till I was pressing into her. I saw her hand move behind me as she shut the door to the shower tightly.

"HA! I win!" As she grabbed the soap off of the ledge I realized that she had tricked me and my head and tail lifted in defiance of her, snorting at her laughter I pressed my head into her chest as my tail started wagging. I had a strange urge to do something but before I could process my whole body started doing a huge doggy shake soaking her more than the shower already had. Her mouth had opened when her eyes closed as she gasped from being soaked. Wiping her face with her hand she squirted a pile of shampoo in her hand and started rubbing it all over my back. Her hand hit a sweet spot that made my foot start shaking uncontrollably at her touch causing her to snort out a loud giggle. Blowing a puff of air at her with my nose she bent down and kissed between my eyes.

"I Love you Tara LaRenge. In all of your goofiness you will always be my number one." She smiled as my tail started to wag again.

I sat down on my haunches and let her clean my chest and under my feet, her expert fingers pulled out twigs and mud from my paws and fur while her other hand cleaned in my ears. With a chuckle she removed the showerhead from its holder and started the rinsing process. Once all the soap had finally gotten off of me I shook once again causing her peals of laughter to echo around the small room. Turning uncomfortably till my nose was pressed to the shower door I pawed pitifully at it to be let out. Shaking her head with a sigh she opened the door for me and I scrambled out waiting by the bathroom door with excitement. I wanted to run and roll around to get my extra energy out, I started barking joyfully and pawing at the door.

"Hold your horses! You need to be toweled off before you go running like a crazy dog!" Grabbing a giant fluffy towel off the rack she tossed it over my head blocking out my vision. Her hands rubbed back and forth trying to get the excess water out of my fur. When she was finally done and had removed the towel I shook again spraying excess droplets all over the place. As soon as her hand reached the doorknob and opened it I was out like a shot from a gun, circling the tiny cabin up and down the hallway and back and forth from the chairs to the couch. Jeremy had been cleaned off too and was sitting right next to Tom who was at the stove making a pot of something that smelled amazing. Both of them looked over as I made a fool of myself racing around the room as though my tail was on fire.

Jeremy came padding over to where I had started rolling back and forth on my back and started nipping at my paws. Both of us began barking and biting at each other as he chased me around the room. Zoey wandered out of the bathroom with a towel around her body and a very harassed look on her face.

"Did you have fun?" Tom said in a singsong voice sweetly. Stopping my pursuit of Jeremy I looked over at Zoey and cocked my head to the side wondering the same thing. Her eyes narrowed at him as she shook her head and went to our bedroom.

Following after her I walked into the room as she was slipping pajamas I had never seen before on. They had little paw prints all over as a design with a matching T-shirt that said 'Who let the dogs out' on the front of it. Giving me a tight lipped smile she slipped into bed under the covers and curled up on her side. My ears fell as I padded over to the bed and nudged her hand. As she gazed at me her fingers slid through my fur gently.

"I'm okay, just really tired from all the stuff happening lately." her mouth opened in a huge yawn and I noticed her fangs hadn't gone away. Tilting my head to the side I licked her neck lightly and nudged her mouth.

"What?" I gave her a knowing look. "I'm fine I just haven't fed for a little while is all. I'll be fine." when she said that my ears perked up.

Running to the other side of the bed I lept onto it sending pillows flying as I jumped up and down. Sitting up she looked at me as though I was insane.

Chapter 17

Little Things

—⁓∘⌀⌀⌀⌀∘⁓—

<u>Zoey</u>

Tara had lept onto the bed sending all the pillows flying off in different directions, as she kept jumping up and down I could feel my annoyance building up. I hadn't fed in about two days and she was really testing my patience. The beast before me rolled onto her back and exposed her neck to me, looking at me with her intelligent eyes.

"I just wanna sleep Tara. I'm tired, I haven't fed since we left, and I am a little pissy right now. Can you please go play with Jeremy or Tom?" her ears plastered themselves to the top of her head again as she started whining at me. "How many times do I need to tell you? I. AM. NOT. HAVING. SEX. WITH. AN. ANIMAL." I punctuated each word with an angry glare. We stubbornly stared at each other when she opened her mouth and started barking and yelping as though she were talking. Gripping the bridge of my nose I let out a sigh and looked at the clock, it was only after midnight. Tired of arguing I looked at her. "What did you have in mind?" I could feel the bruises under my eyes getting deeper every passing second. She sat down on the bed lightly and tilted her head up, giving me the side eye as though she wanted me to mimic her.

"What? This? This is what you want?" I tilted my head to the side and looked up exposing my neck to her. Within a second her jaws were around my throat causing me to freeze up in shock. Before I could do or say anything though she had let me go and exposed her neck to me again. A few seconds passed before her strange display clicked in my tired brain.

"You want me to bite you?" she snorted at me in affirmation.

"No sex right? No strings attached?" another snort. "Well…" thinking about it for a moment she began whining "Fuck it, what the hell." Lifting myself out from the covers I got on my knees as she laid herself down and eyeballed me. Frowning at her display I felt the familiar burning sensation in my stomach as the venom filled my mouth up. Leaning down to her neck I peeked over at her face. She was staring out the window with a calm expression as though she was waiting on a train to arrive.

Taking a deep breath I imagined my human Tara laying in front of me with her neck exposed and her breasts as perky as ever, gingerly fingering herself waiting on me to strike. That did the trick, my instincts kicked in and I had struck into her neck and tapped the vein perfectly. Her blood was filling my mouth as I drank deeply, the only betrayal of Tara's calm demeanor was her ears against her head and her tail between her legs. A light whimpering came out from her mouth as I continued to drink my fill, causing my resolve to falter a little bit. Her back leg had begun shaking lightly as I sucked, I placed my hand on her flank and began petting her lightly to keep her calm. Finding the spot that sent her leg into a kicking frenzy I began scratching at it till her foot was making helicopter noises along the comforter. When I had drank my fill my fangs slowly returned back into my mouth and I licked the wound closed so she wouldn't bleed out. Sitting up from her I patted her head easily.

"Thank you for that." I could already feel the bruises under my eyes disappearing as her blood worked through me, I slipped back under the covers as she sat up and watched me. Looking at the beautiful animal in front of me I felt almost bad that I couldn't do anything for her. Patting the bed next to me I smiled and laid down as she curled into a ball by my side. Her eyes drooped closed as she snuggled closely to me.

Chapter 18
Wild Things

_____~w~o~c~e~t~o~c~t~o~o~w~_____

<u>Tara</u>

I woke up alone in the bed where I had laid next to Zoey all through the night stretching I yawned deeply curling and uncurling my toes. Looking around the room I smelled Zoey's scent on the pillows and my body responded with a pleasurable tightness. Getting off the bed I padded over to my suitcase and slipped on pajama pants and a top I tucked the necklace Zoey had given me for my birthday into my shirt and walked into the living room and looked around. Zoey was at the breakfast bar chatting happily with Tom over his cooking style. Quiet as a ghost I snuck up behind her and hugged her to me while kissing her neck softly and giving her little nibbles along her jaw line. I saw Tom out of the corner of my eye peek over and drop the hot pan he had been using on the floor in shock. The crashing noise caused me to look up at him.

"Was it too hot for you Tom?" my voice was strange and warped as though it was between a growl and words. Zoey froze under my touch and I saw her head turn slowly to look at me as her eyes widened in panic, I looked around for the source of the danger. "What's wrong guys?" I frowned at my voice again.

"Tara, sweetie... You may want to go get Jeremy." Tom had found his voice first "He should be outside cleaning up the... trophy you guys brought us last night..." Letting Zoey go I frowned at both of them and shook my head. Walking to the door I opened it and saw Jeremy with the garden hose spraying down the concrete where the deer had been. I began walking over to him.

"Hey Jeremy, Tom and Zoey are acting weird and wanted me to come find you." I laughed lightly and it sounded like a pack of hyenas causing Jeremy's head to turn quickly. His eyes widened in shock as he dropped the hose and threw his hands up in front of himself in a submissive manner.

"Tara? W-What would you like me to do?" his eyes turned the deep chocolate brown again as he released his wolf out. I could feel eyes boring into the back of my head as Zoey and Tom watched out of the open door.

"What do you mean? Tom sent me out here to come find you?" I cautiously took a step forward as Jeremy tripped over himself and fell into the mud. He stayed down showing me his neck and belly while keeping his hands open and non aggressive like he did last night. "What's everyone's problem? Why are you all acting so weird?" I turned to Tom and Zoey in the doorway who both took a few steps back. "Zoey?" her head was shaking in disbelief at me.

"Tara?" Jeremy's voice called to me. Turning to look at him his eyes were still the deep brown color as he stared at me. "H-Have you looked in the mirror yet?" I rolled my eyes at his question

"No I got up got dressed and came out to see these two this morning. Why? Do I have twigs or something in my hair?" reaching up to the top of my head I felt two very tall furry things sticking out from my skull. Frowning I looked at my hands and noticed that my nails had turned to pointed spikes. Looking at Zoey I saw the look of panic in her face mirroring my own. Running at a sprint towards them I raced into the bathroom flipped on the light and screamed loud enough to wake the dead. My hands flew to my mouth trying to muffle the scream that kept bubbling up through my lips. Leaning close to the mirror a monster stared back at me.

My reflection showed a wolf like nose with golden yellow eyes and extremely sharp pointed teeth my body had a light peach fuzz all over me with dark brown wolf ears on my head. Reaching out I touched the mirror to make sure it wasn't a trick, my heart was pounding at the sight of myself. Out of the corner of my eye, I saw everyone in the doorway of the bathroom.

"W-What's happened to me?" I asked wildly at Jeremy who unintentionally cowered back from my gaze. He couldn't even lift his head to properly look at me.

"I-I'm not sure." he said sinking lower behind Tom trying to avoid my stare.

"I look like a movie monster!" Checking my teeth again in the mirror it looked like the mouth of a doberman pinscher, my nose was a leathery almost black color just like a dog's.

"What do I do Jeremy!?" I screamed at him in frustration. Zoey who had been silent this whole time walked over to me and reached to touch my face, as soon as her hand made contact I felt a shiver go through my spine. My hand cupped hers to my cheek as she gazed sadly at me.

"Don't worry baby, we can fix this. Maybe it's just a side effect of the full moon and you being an alpha?" she gave me a dazzling smile that warmed my skin. Slowly I felt myself relaxing into her hand when she leaned up to kiss me I felt my eyes close as I hugged her to my body.

Making my way down her neck I nibbled lightly till she gasped in pleasure when I found her favorite spot. I saw Jeremy and Tom out of the corner of my eye wander off into the kitchen. Grabbing Zoey by the hips I lifted her onto my waist so she could hold on and ran us into the bedroom slamming the door behind us. Tossing her lightly on the bed I loomed over her and felt my eyes glowing with passion and wanting for her. Yanking my shirt and pants off I jumped on top of her and grabbed her hands to pin them above her head. A low rumbling growl built up in my chest as I nuzzled her neck while she squirmed under me in excitement.

"I'm gonna make you scream." I whispered quietly in her ear as I made my way down her collarbone and to her t-shirt. Slowly I pulled off her top and sat down on her hips just staring down at her lovely breasts. Putting my head between them I nibbled my way over to the first nipple I saw and started worshiping it. My fingers began pinching lightly on her freed nipple causing her to moan and squirm in ecstasy.

Slowly making my way down her body I loved on every square inch of her till she was mewing in need. Stopping at the hemline of her pants and underwear I looked up at her sweaty brow as she studied me with hooded eyes and lust. Pulling everything off of her I stared at the beauty before me and began licking and suckeling till her skin was pink and swollen with excitement.

Grabbing the toy from the bedside I slipped the holder into myself and before either one of us were ready I had rammed into her causing her to scream out my name loudly with a mix of obscenities. A gut wrenching growl had begun building up in me once again as I pounded into her like a beast. Our sweat mingling heavily as my musk overtook all odors of the room sliding in and out of her folds our pressure was building enough to cause her to climax as she screamed again as though she was being murdered. I continued my movements till she had stilled beneath me, my hips slowing down to a slow rocking pace as I circled inside her.

"Was that okay?" I asked her. "I'm sorry, I can't-" my hips had started working again on their own, causing me to resume my motions. "I can't s-stop" my legs began quivering with excitement as I felt her pleasure start to build once again. Her hands flew to my face holding me completely still.

"Don't stop then." She kissed me deeply and released as my hips resumed their pendulum movements. Grabbing her by the hips I yanked out of her and flipped her to her stomach ramming into her from behind like a bitch in heat. After about four more hours and countless orgasms later we were both sated and sleepy, her body pressed closely to mine as we hugged each other I would wake every so often to lick under her neck or to nibble her breast to keep her sated. A knock on the door disturbed us. Throwing a blanket over us both we yelled for the intruder to enter.

Jeremy peeked around the corner, his nostrils flared out and his eyes turned a deep brown again as he took in the smell of musk in the room. "I-I wanted to let you know the moon will be rising at 8:15pm tonight...:" he scrambled out after letting me know his message while closing the door back.

Looking down at Zoey I saw her perky breasts teasing the covers with how erect they were. Blowing a puff of air at her I laid on my back and pulled her atop me till she was positioned where she would wanna be. Her eyes lit up with excitement as she grasped the dildo firmly in her hand and slid all the way down to the base where our pubic hair was tangling together.

As I watched her please herself on the toy my hands trailed up to her hip bones as she picked up speed. Looking in her eyes I smiled as her head rolled back on her neck and her mouth opened to reveal her neat little points on her fangs. The faster she worked the toy the harder it would press into me building my pleasure up higher and higher till we were both matched in pace. Her arms bent backwards to hold onto my thighs as her breasts forced themselves forward straining against the pressure between us. As we continued I felt a deep primal build of our climax coming to a close, grabbing her hips I shoved the toy deep into her in a final surge as we broke each other. Her scream of pleasure and my howl of ecstasy mingled and hung in the air between us till she fell forward onto my chest breathing heavily. Kissing the top of her head I began petting her back gently and nuzzling her ear till she stirred from her reverie with a deep throaty sigh to lean up and kiss me as I removed the toy from us.

"That. was. Fantastic." Zoey sighed with pleasure "Maybe you should get stuck like this more often." she mumbled sleepily as I chuckled deeply in my throat. Looking at the ceiling I put one arm under my head and rubbed her back in slow gentle motions. Dozing off my brain threw out the thought *MINE* once again.

My little nap was disturbed by immense pain cutting through me causing my body to buck and seize throwing Zoey off with a yelp. My screams became muffled as I turned over on my belly to bite the pillow under my head, my skin was crawling with unseen creatures under them as my muscles and bones regrew and began snapping in two and healing over again. The thick fur coated my whole body as my tail shot out and grew plump and furry. Howling in pain my back snapped as my mouth elongated to a snout causing me to fall onto the bed in a heap. Breathing heavily the necklace she had bought me had fallen to the floor from slipping off of my head. I stayed on my side laying down as I heard Zoey walk around to stand in front of me. Her hand touched my paw lightly, they were almost the same size as each other's. Reaching down with her other hand she grabbed the necklace and tossed it into my open suitcase.

"You okay?" the concern was evident in her voice as I focused on my breathing. My tail however gave me away as it started pounding on the bed like a drummer. Smiling she pet my head lightly and kissed between my eyes, before she could pull away I stole a kiss from her with a long sloppy dog tongue licking her from her chin to raising her bangs to stand in odd angles.

"Ew! God don't do that!" her laughter made me snort loudly. Getting up from my position I stretched my feet down to the floor till I was standing on all fours in front of her. My head reached just below her breasts so just a little over 3.5 feet tall. Looking at Zoey expectantly I padded my way to the door waiting for her to open it for me. Once she did I ran around the room and hopped up onto the couch in excitement causing Tom to spill his bowl of popcorn all over the floor.

"FUCK!...." he shot me a glare "At least you're feeling better I suppose… Zoey get her outside before she breaks something." Zoey wandered to the door and opened it to reveal a perfect night. Bounding over the furniture I raced out the door only to be tackled down by Jeremy who had planned a sneak attack on me causing us to tumble in a mass of fur and teeth as we snapped and chomped at each other. As he wiggled out from under me I heard Zoey yell from the door.

"Be safe! I'm looking forward to a morning like this one again!" she waved at me from the door. Barking an affirmation at her I raced after Jeremy into the thicket to continue our game of chase.

The game went on for a good forty to fifty minutes before I had become bored with it. Looking around I noticed a pillar of smoke bubbling over the tree line. Barking at Jeremy to come find me I began wandering towards the source of the smoke. I smelled food cooking and the noise of people talking in hushed rumbling voices. Jeremy found me and was by my side and was listening to the conversations the humans were having.

"I hope we can find these damn wolves soon, they have a pretty penny for them to be brought in and sold." the first voice mumbled over what I assumed was food.

"My sources said that they were suppose to come up this way for the full moon, so I'm sure we will get them, just gotta keep an eye out for them." the second voice was much deeper than the first

Jeremy started backing up and snapped a twig under his back foot. My head spun around to look at him with an oh shit face, the men had gone silent from their conversation spinning my whole body around I bit at Jeremy's flank causing him to yelp as we started running from the site. I could hear the men's boots crashing through the underbrush and leaves as they trailed behind us. I let out a long warning howl while I was running to alert Tom and Zoey that something was wrong. Catching up with Jeremy I bit him again forcing him to run faster. The noise of a gun clicking had sent my feet into a frenzy as I zigzagged through the trees trying to lose the hunters from our trail. A small prick hit my flank causing me to stumble and yelp. Picking myself up from the ground I raced faster back to the cabin and saw Jeremy making his way inside with Tom blocking the door. Urging me faster I tumbled into the living room as the door slammed behind me and locked. Whimpering pathetically my tail curled between my legs as I felt my head loll off to the side. Trying to keep my eyes open I saw Zoey standing over me and examining where I had been hit, she pulled a little red dart out of my rear and tossed it into the fire before examining the rest of me. When she touched my front right paw I snapped my teeth at her and whimpered.

"Baby what happened? Who did this to you?" her eyes glowed an evil angry purple color causing her fangs to pop out. Looking at Tom he helped carry me to the bedroom as my vision faded in and out from the drugs they shot at me. Jeremy hopped next to me on the bed and laid his head on my neck in comfort while whining. Zoey grabbed a gauze bandage and a stick from our fire starting pile and wrapped my foot up in a splint. A pounding noise came from the front door as she finished.

"Stay here. You too Jeremy." closing the door behind her we both stayed silent awaiting a sign of danger.

Zoey

WHO THE FUCK DO THEY THINK THEY ARE MESSING WITH MY BABY PUPPY! My anger was monumental as I started walking to the door. Tom stood in my way and whispered in my ear to go into the bathroom and calm down before I did anything stupid. I heard his voice talking with what sounded like two men asking about giant dogs running through here and how they were his. Tom handled it beautifully till I heard a crash from the bedroom window.

Throwing open the door to the bathroom I burst into the bedroom to see Jeremy on top of another man in all black whose gun had been ripped from his now severed hand. The noise of a fight breaking out in the living room sent me running to help when I heard another screaming yelp from the bedroom as a fourth man had Tara and was dragging her out the window as she was thrashing. Leaping over Jeremy and the other man I tackled the brute who had my baby and went for his throat. Sinking my teeth into his neck his blood was spicy and sweet giving me a surge of pleasure as he dropped to the ground like a sack of bricks. Tara was trying to get up from falling out of his arms but every movement would cause her to whimper and cry out in pain.

Racing to her side I pulled her over to the bushes under the window. "Stay here and stay quiet my love, I have to help Tom." kissing her forehead I ran over to the front door and grabbed the nearest man and twisted his neck till his throat exposed where I bit as hard as possible and drained him within four seconds flat. Tom had the other one in a headlock on the ground holding tightly till he had struggled so much that a thick crack reverberated around the room snapping his neck.

"SHIT! I was trying to save him for questioning… Where's Tara and Jeremy!?" He asked in a panic. I explained where they were and then raced out the door to make sure she was still under the window. What I saw stopped me dead.

Tara was being loaded into a black SUV by 3 more guys in black when Jeremy flew through the window and bit the hand off of one of them while he dove for the throat of another, two of the three dropped like stones as the last one took aim and fired a stake I heard Tara's horrible yelping screech as the wood entered right through my sternum. I saw Jeremy rip his head off as I fell backwards into the grass.

Chapter 19

Lost

Tara

I saw the stake fly from the man's crossbow as it hit Zoey my heart stopped. I dragged myself out of the van and limped over to her body every step causing me horrible pain I whimpered and licked her face trying to get a reaction from her. The face that I had loved so much, the voice I heard in my dreams. All of it was gone now, her pealing laughter and sense of humor was gone. Staring blankly at the sky forever. I curled next to her and felt my body sobbing as I let out a long mournful cry, a mix of a scream and a howl. My mate was gone.

I.

Was.

Gone.

My head laid upon her breast as the darkness consumed me to where I didn't have to think anymore…

Chapter 20

Love

<u>Zoey</u>

My whole body was paralyzed from the stake it hurt. I could only see and hear what was going on around me. The noises terrified me, the loud scream of Tara's wolf scared me more than anything, I saw her lick at my face and cry out to the sky at her thinking I was dead. My body refused to move as her head laid on my chest as she passed out on top of me crying in pain and loss. Her howl would haunt me for the rest of my unnatural life.

I saw Tom walk over to me as he looked down at us, tears had filled his eyes as he swallowed hard and gripped the stake. Yanking with all his might he pulled the fucker out of me sending a jolt of pain reverberating all around my body causing me to suck in a deep breath.

"OW MOTHER FUCKER!" my head fell back onto the ground as my cells began curling in around themselves to repair the damage done by the horrible piece of wood. With a sigh I looked down at Tara and saw her paw had twisted at an odd angle as she had curled into me. Petting her lightly I noticed her splint was nowhere in sight.

Tom let out a chuckle and lifted her off of me as carefully as possible. "She really does love you." walking her into the house I slowly stood as Jeremy helped nudge me up to a standing position. My chest was gonna take a while to fix itself. Wandering into the bedroom I shared with Tara I laid down next to her curled up form and held her tightly to me for comfort. I laid there for hours watching her chest move up and down.

Only when the light from the morning came through the window did her body seamlessly change back to her human form, no more halfway stuck it seemed. Her body moved slowly till she was facing me in a deep slumber. Her right hand had swollen twice its size and looked as though she had sprained it. Looking at the ceiling I pulled her close to me and had no dreams or nightmares for a few peaceful hours while we slept.

Tara

I woke up too warm under the covers and my wrist was pounding in pain. The fog had started lifting from my brain and I prayed that it would come back so I wouldn't have to face the day. My shoulders shook as I silently sobbed into the pillow and hugged myself tight. Zoey was dead, Zoey was gone. Her body was on the ground in a heap. Her soft skin turned to marble, her eyes staring open for eternity. I felt bile rising up my throat so fast that I bent over the edge of the bed and retched everything that was in my stomach from the past three days. The acid burned my throat till a cool hand brushed my hair back from my face.

"You're okay sweetheart, don't worry." Zoey's voice penetrated the room I was hearing things now. I sobbed harder and retched again with nothing but bile coming up. I could almost feel her sitting next to me rubbing my back. If this was a dream I didn't want it to end. I hugged the apparition closer to me in hopes of making the pain go away sobbing into its chest.

"Please… Please don't leave me." my voice was choked up as I ugly cried all over myself as snot dripped out my nose.

"Tara. Tara look at me baby." a pair of cold hands raise my face up to look into the face of my love.

"Am I dead too?" tears streamed down my face in horrible wet streaks all down my cheeks. The phantom raised its eyebrow at me and pinched my right wrist causing me to yelp in pain. "WHAT THE FUCK!" with a gasp I looked into Zoey's eyes "you're alive?" my voice came out in a whisper.

"Sweetheart I never died! It takes a lot more than a stake to take down a vampire, you gotta lob our heads off to do any real damage!" Hugging me closely I breathed in her smell and sobbed harder into her. My breathing hitched every couple of seconds catching on itself.

We talked for an hour after that when Jeremy and Tom

announced that we would be returning home. They had called the cleaning crew to get rid of the bodies and to dispose of the SUV they were gonna take us with. Gingerly we were brought to the car and seated in the back as gently as possible while we never let eachother go. Jeremy said we would all hang out with our spouses tonight instead of going out for another run with those people actually looking for us. I snuggled next to Zoey all the way home. We had stopped and gotten Atlas from the daycare and wandered up to our apartment. Opening the door we gingerly walked ourselves to the bedroom where we laid in each other's arms for a good while.

I examined her chest where the stake had went in and been pulled out and was able to watch the progress of it healing well. My wrist had begun healing, we had wrapped an ace bandage around it since there was really no use getting a cast for how fast a wolf heals. I looked into Zoey's eyes and kissed her often, so often that we would have to stop for air and bathroom breaks.

Around midday we came together for a sweet coupling of our bodies intertwining, very slow and steady with nothing rushed and everything perfectly joining up. By the end of it we were reveling in the enjoyment of each other's company. When the sun started to set she had put a very large collar around my throat with a leash dangling from it in case I tried to fly the coop again.

Giving her a quick peck on the lips before she walk out of the room, I sat at the foot of the bed on the floor and waited for the change to take hold of me. I could feel the tension curl in my toes as my body began transforming into the powerful brown black wolf. The pain was astronomical as my bones snapped and regrew tenfold my wrist began throbbing painfully before being replaced by normal bones once again. My back arched up in release as the final crack settled everything into place. I quickly shook myself out as I stood gracefully on all fours, when the bright blue leash caught my eye. Gently I picked it up between my teeth and padded to the door and scratched lightly till I heard footsteps walking towards me. My tail wagged as Zoey opened the door to allow me to leave the bedroom, snorting my thank you at her I wandered to the living room and hopped up on the couch letting the leash fall out of my mouth as I rested my head on my front paws successfully taking up two full couch cushions. Zoey wandered over to the free space and laid on top of me using my body as a giant fluffy pillow.

"Anything you wanna watch on tv?" she smiled at me as she reached for the remote. Giving her the side eye I gave her an innocent wide eyed look. "My choice? Perfect." when I snorted she giggled and flipped on the Tv. while browsing the channels Atlas wandered over to us and began sniffing my paws that were hanging off the couch with curiosity. I watched the little pup wander over to the front door and paw at it demanding to go outside. Giving Zoey a sideways glance I snorted at her. When she looked up she laughed.

"I guess you can't exactly take him out can you?" Getting up off of me she walked to the door where I followed closely behind her. When she reached up to grab his leash I nudged my head into her butt and presented my leash to her. "What you wanna go out too?" when I let off a quiet bark she rolled her eyes at me.

"Fine but if I get dragged all the way down to 5th avenue I'm gonna be pissed." As she reached down to grab my leash I gave her a sloppy kiss all up her cheek. "Ew! I told you to stop doing that! Atlas has enough sense not to give me kisses like that why don't you?" with a sigh she hooked him up and opened the door. I stopped at the top of the stairs and frowned slightly.

Oh right… stairs…

slowly I took one step at a time trying to keep my balance on the way down while Zoey laughed at me the whole time.

"Bigbaby." shesnickeredatme. AswemadeitoutsideIgotthedistinct smell of *garbagehobopigeonpoopchinesefoodasphaltcarexhaust* it made my head spin with the possibilities of what was to come. Tugging on the leash I wandered down the street with Atlas and Zoey in tow stopping every so often to smell something interesting. When we made it to a little green space called the 'dog park' we wandered around till Atlas found a little tree to piss on where he then wiped his feet kicking up grass behind himself. Looking up at Zoey she was eyeballing me expectantly. Frowning at her expression I snorted at her like she was crazy and went to turn around before she tugged my leash again.

"I'm not gonna let you piss in the house, think you're gonna be able to hold it that long?" She grinned at me when I snorted at her again in annoyance. We started walking back to the apartment and made it back into the living room where she unhooked both of us. Atlas wandered over to the little dog bed in the corner as I hopped back onto the couch and laid down as Zoey positioned herself behind me once again.

As we channel hopped Zoey settled on a documentary of the egyptian pyramids. She cuddled closely to me and I felt her breathing slow as she drifted off to sleep, nudging her head I hopped off the couch causing her to jerk awake. Looking around sleepily I grabbed her pant leg and tugged lightly till she followed me into the bedroom where I pushed her onto the bed and hopped up next to her. As I stretched out I nuzzled into her neck and drifted to sleep right after her.

Chapter 21

Stuck

<u>Zoey</u>

I woke up to an empty bed and the curtains drawn blocking out any light that may come in, I heard the noise of a large animal running around my apartment while Atlas barked excitedly. Getting up I threw my mandala robe on again and wandered to the living room to see the commotion. Tara still in wolf form had Atlas's pull and tug toy in her mouth and was teasing him by dangling it just out of reach when he would run to grab it causing him to bark excitedly.

When she looked up from her game he grabbed it and raced around the apartment with his prize. As she padded over to me in greeting she nuzzled my hand and licked between my fingers and looked to the window where the sun was shining brightly in the kitchen. Blinking a few times I frowned down at her.

"You didn't change back yet?" I asked in a worried tone, when she shook her head I looked around the room and found my phone sitting on the edge of the side table. Dialing up Tom's number I let it ring a few times before calling again where he picked up on the second ring.

"BITCH DO YOU KNOW WHAT TIME IT IS?!" his voice screamed out at me from the phone.

"Good morning to you too Tom, has Jeremy changed back to normal yet?" I asked sweetly.

"Yeah he changed when the moon f-fell." he said with a yawn.

"That's great! But I have two dogs running around my apartment this morning instead of just one." I said in a singsong voice. "So if you two would be so kind as to get your bums over here that would be great please."

"Right we will be right over. Jeremy get up, no not that up, well maybe later, no it's Tara. Your cousin? Yeah Tara, She hasn't changed back yet we have to go. We'll be there in about 10 minutes" he said before hanging up.

Looking down at Tara I smiled. "Jeremy and Tom will be here soon they will fix us right up." her head tilted to the side as her tail started wagging lightly.

Walking to the bedroom I dressed myself and brushed my hair out so I looked halfway decent, the whole time Tara was staring at me like a slab of meat occasionally giving off little moans and barks while her nose sniffed the air around me.

"What?" I asked finally looking at her as she tilted her head to the side giving me puppy dog eyes. "Do you need to... go potty or something?" when she whined I rolled my eyes and walked to get her leash, only to hear her padding into the bathroom. Swinging back to peek in on her she had lifted the toilet seat up and was waiting on me to leave again. "Make sure you put the seat down..." I said as someone knocked on the door. Walking through the living room I opened the door to reveal Jeremy and Tom standing there waiting to be let in. Both looked as though they had just crawled out of bed and neither one looked happy about it.

"Where is she?" Jeremy asked as they walked in and wandered into the living room.

"She's uh... well she's using the toilet." I said with as straight of a face as I could muster. Both of them looked at me with utter shock as they glanced at each other before Tom burst out laughing.

"Girl you need to film that and put it on youtube!" Tom laughed so hard that his pot belly jiggled. When Jeremy and I shot him an annoyed glare he clammed up and awkwardly coughed. "Right, girlfriend and cousin."

I rolled my eyes at Jeremy as we walked over to the couch and all patiently waited for her to come out. Right after the toilet flushed we heard the sound of the lid falling to the bowl and Tom gave me an amused grin out of the corner of his mouth as Tara walked into the living room to sit at my feet. Jeremy stood up and walked to sit on the floor in front of her and began examining her closely.

When he touched the collar he jerked his hand back quickly yelping loudly. His hand had begun changing into a clawed

159

paw causing him to hold it gingerly in pain. When he backed up a bit his hand had started returning to normal again.

"Well there's your problem!" Tom said happily. "What's that thing made of? Silver?" I looked at the collar and frowned.

"Um, possibly? I got it at the ritzy boutique a few weeks ago, I figured it would be a good thing to have around if she went haywire again." I grabbed the collar and began taking it off of her.

"Silver reveals the beast within. For werewolves anyway. That's how hunters back in the day would find us, they would shoot us with one silver bullet so we wouldn't be able to change back till we got it out of our systems. Once the poison was gone we could return to normal." Jeremy explained. "Though that's also how the wolfman stories came up, if we wear little things like jewelry with silver in it we go into half form. That could be why Tara couldn't change back before when we were at the cabin. She had the necklace you gave her on didn't she? That explains the whole stuck thing too." as we were talking Tara raced to the bedroom and I heard the distinct noise of her pained growls as she changed back to human form. After a few minutes she appeared in the bedroom doorway completely normal wearing my mandala robe and looking like death warmed over. She rushed over to Jeremy and hugged him tightly.

"Thank you guys so much I was getting so tired of not having a voice!" she then switched over to Tom who wrapped her into a bear hug.

"Not a problem sweetie, just next time you have an issue can you like call closer to noon instead of oh 7am?" Tom said with a laugh. As they both got up from their chairs Tara stood next to me and grinned at them as they left. When I closed the door I felt her arms snake around my waist as she hugged me to her tightly. Leading me to the bedroom we found ourselves on the bed as we kissed passionately a small string of spit connecting our mouths. Before we got further however I stopped our progression before we got too heated.

"Hey, do you think... maybe we could have you wear the necklace I bought you?" I smiled shyly up at her. A slow smile spread over her mouth as she got up off of me. Reaching over my head she pulled the necklace off of the bedpost where it had been hanging since we had arrived home yesterday and slipped it around her neck.

Tara laid back against the pillows as her skin started to lightly shimmer in the morning light. We locked eyes as they changed from her beautiful blue to a deep golden yellow. Her face had smaller changes while her ears began moving upward till they were atop her head as her nose blackened to resemble leather, the hair on her body turned to a dark brown peach fuzz as it sprung up everywhere. Her mouth parted slightly revealing sharp pointed teeth. With a throaty growl her transformation was finished as she stared at me with hungry eyes as though she wanted to devour me.

Her hands slowly reached up and grabbed my face and pressed her lips to my own while she caressed my cheeks with her pointed claws dragging them slowly over my neck.

"Is this what you wanted?" her voice had once again warped into the throaty growl. "You like me like this?" her eyes glowed brightly staring at me. As her hand made it down past my collar bone and rubbed my breasts through my shirt I gasped and nodded eagerly. Her clawed hands slipped their way under my top and bra till they found my nipples.

"YES!" I shivered with anticipation as her nails swirled around my areola causing them to throb in a deliciously painful way. Her fingers spun the rings that I had put in place of the bars I had in earlier. Her gravelly voice purred in my ear.

"These are new." her eyes shined as she clicked her nails against the metal. "I like them." I felt my legs begin scissoring as she tugged and pulled at the rings teasing them with her nails. Tara made a throaty growl of approval as her nose flared out finding my scent causing her pupils to dilate till they took up most of her iris.

Pulling her face down to mine our lips connected as a sizzle of electricity spiked through our pleasure she raised her knee up to press it against my sex, as she rolled it back and forth over my jeans the fiction sent shivers coursing through my spine.

Tara's hands moved from my breasts till she made her way to my ass. The light pressure of her nails digging into my rear sent me spiralling out into waves of exhilaration as her knee kept working between my legs. My moans were getting louder and more needy with each passing second. When her hands unbuttoned my jeans her robe fell open revealing her soft pillowy breasts. Leaning into her chest I took her nipple into my mouth and began sucking lightly. As she arched and gasped I used my free hand to play with the other one, her moan of approval urged me onward as I nibbled lightly she yanked my pants past my knees and grabbed my sex in her hand rubbing her palm in a circular motion before using her nail to slice the thin fabric in half.

"Hey! Those were new..." I cried out in displeasure, as she slid her fingers into me my protests were silenced as I moaned loudly falling into her neck. I could feel her heated breath in my ear.

"I'll buy you the whole fucking store." she gruffly moaned as her fingers danced inside of me. "You're so perfect... I want you forever as mine." Nibbling my ear her voice became breathy as I rode harder on her hand. "Marry Me." With a gasp I froze on the upswing and looked down at her.

"A-Are you serious?" I felt my mouth hanging open in shock but I didn't care. For the first time I really looked at the beautiful wolf woman I was sitting on top of, whose fingers were jammed so far up into me that I would be able to sing soprano if I tried. Her eyes gleamed in the morning sun as she gazed at me in wonder. Her glossy hair or fur whatever form she was in, the way she mourned over me when she thought I had passed on, all of our firsts together, especially our first kiss, the taste of her skin when she pleasures herself. Everything about her always screams love, how could I ever say no to her.

"Of course I'm serious..." Uncertainty flitted across her face as she started frowning, I felt her fingers pull out of me gently as her eyes searched my face.

R.J. Young

"YES!" hugging her close to me her arms wrapped around me pressing our bodies closer together. In a surge I was flipped onto my back as she took control above me, she had pulled the robe off of herself as it pooled around her knees. Grabbing my rear she slowly pushed me back till I was sitting up against the headboard, as she smiled she laid a hand on each of my legs and began spreading them till my folds were open and exposed to the light chill of the room.

As she leaned down she planted a kiss on my neck she left little nibbles all down my body till she made it right past my navel. Her hand swiftly found my pubic hair and began gliding her nails gently over the dusting of curls there. Looking at me from her position she smiled long and slowly as her eyes began glowing a deeper gold. Slowly sliding down she kissed above the hair and glided her tongue all the way down till she found and stimulated my clitoris gently at first then picking up speed till it became almost painful, as she moved further downward her tongue suddenly became a ribbon dancer as she twirled it in and out of me with such precision I could swear she had eyes in her mouth. As I rode her mouth faster that tongue of hers picked up speed, my arms reached for her head pressing her closer to me. I felt my skin begin to burn as she sucked my sex harder. When her fingers dove into me as deep as she could go it was my undoing. Crying out to the sky in passion my back arched one final time as I slid backwards onto the pillows and passed out.

Chapter 22

Love

—◇◇◇◇◇◇◇◇◇◇—

<u>Tara</u>

Raising up from between Zoey's legs I looked over her beautiful form and kissed her between her folds one last time before getting off the bed. I grabbed the robe at my feet and wrapped it around myself after I covered her up with a blanket to keep her warm. Walking over to the bathroom I shut the door quietly behind myself I walked over to the full body mirror and let the robe fall to the ground. Blinking at the beast in front of me I looked at myself, my whole body was covered in a dark brown almost black fuzz that matched my ears that were protruding out from the top of my head. My nose was almost like leather as my face had half formed to a muzzle shape my sharpened teeth poked out from over my lip giving me a slight overbite, my golden eyes stared back at me as I examined myself. Looking at the necklace around my neck the silver glinted in the light off of the chain sending little reflections around my chest. Slowly taking it off I felt my body begin to shift back uncomfortably till I looked like a normal human again except for my golden eyes.

Once I placed the chain on the counter and stepped back my eyes returned to their boring blue color. I wandered over to the tub and began filling it with hot water, once it reached the halfway point I poured in bubble bath and let the foamy clouds form till it was like jumping into a giant cotton ball. Gently I stepped into the water and grabbed my Ipod off of the vanity, pressing play I slipped the earbuds into my ears and relaxed my head back against the cool ceramic. Breathing in deeply I enjoyed just floating in the water relaxing as best as possible. It had been one hell of a weekend and I was utterly spent, being with Zoey was fantastic but it can get exhausting with all the sex.

Slowly I closed my eyes till all I could see were the lyrics dancing in my mind's eye, the slow smooth chorus with the sweet melodies spoke to me on a level I couldn't even put into words. When a hand brushed through my hair however I jumped up sloshing water over the side and right onto Zoey's bare feet. Looking up at her she had on an expression of reverence and enjoyment at seeing my naked form through the bubbles. Removing my earbuds I looked up at her as her hand dipped into the water and skimmed along the top like a figure skater.

"Mind if I join you?" she asked coyly as her fingers teased lightly over my breast. Sitting up a little more I gestured for her to step in with me while offering my hand to her. Gratefully she grasped my offering and stepped lightly into the tub. She turned slowly so she would be sitting with her back to me.

Our bodies touched in the hot water and I felt every inch of her with heightened senses as our skin rubbed against each other, Whitney Houston's I will always love you played through the earbuds as we layed back together into the water as the steam bubbled around us fogging up the air. Laying my head on top of hers we just held onto one another as we soaked. As she took a deep breath she turned her body towards me and smiled my favorite smile.

"You left before I had a chance to please you." her hand slid down my body between my legs when she reached my swollen sex I jerked, causing a large grin to spread across her face. Her hand began teasing my opening as she watched me jump every couple of seconds, causing me to moan when she would hit a sweet spot. My heartbeat began beating fast as she would slide her fingers inside me before pulling them out with a giggle. I felt my eyes begin turning their golden color, reaching between my own legs I grabbed her hand lightly.

"H-Hang on." My tongue had changed to a flat spade shape again causing it to flop out of my mouth. When she gave me a quizzical look I blinked down at her as my eyes changed back to blue. "I... I don't want to change right now. I'm just trying to control it..." my voice had gone breathy explaining my thoughts. Zoey's face clouded in confusion, when she sat up on her knees I looked at her. The air in the room had turned almost chilly from the heat of the tub causing her nipples to go erect when the air hit them.

"Why don't you want to change?" her voice was whispered.

"I-" frowning I thought about it for a moment, the uneasiness of seeing a beast look back when I saw myself in the mirror now, the fear of losing myself one day and hurting her, the panic of not being able to change back. "I just don't okay." my voice had hardened with all of the thoughts racing through my head. I no longer felt relaxed and my pleasure had disappeared like a wisp of smoke. Pulling my legs to me I stood up and grabbed a towel off the rack, I walked out of the bathroom embarrassed at my own thoughts. I heard the tub drain and Zoey's wet footsteps follow me into our bedroom. I dug in my designated drawer and pulled out underwear and a set of pajamas. Not bothering to towel off my hair I slipped the clothing on and walked to bed and curled up under the covers. My mood had soured from her question which upset me more than it should have.

Why can't she understand? I hate not being in control of myself, it scares me, it hurts me.

<u>Zoey</u>

Tara's inner voice swirled around the room the last part struck me especially hard. *It hurts me.* If I had known I wouldn't have asked her to change for my own selfish pleasure. My mouth had gone dry from my selfishness, I walked over to her side of the bed and sat at her feet.

"I'm so sorry Tara… I didn't mean to upset you." her thoughts kept swirling into a dark place as she continued to think about our conversation. I felt my jaw line harden as she stared blankly at the wall her eyes would blink quickly at times but she stayed silent. My hunger interrupted my thoughts as I felt my fangs grow to painful points her neck was exposed so gracefully, almost like a swan.

Ignoring my own urges I got up from the bed and walked into the kitchen and peeked into the mini fridge under the counter. All of the shelves were completely bare of blood bags. Silently cursing to myself I quietly walked to the bedroom and threw on some clothes, Tara didn't budge at any of the noises I made. Walking to the front door I grabbed the doorknob and immediately felt as though I was cheating on her, it burned my chest as my hunger growled out of my throat. Releasing the Knob I walked back to the couch and sat down, staring blankly at the TV that wasn't on.

Hugging my knees to my chest I placed my head down on them and breathed through the hunger pains.

Tara

I wasn't sure how much time had passed when I blinked awake but I remember Zoey coming in before and picking up what I assumed were her clothes that had been scattered around the room. I turned to her side of the bed and realized that she wasn't there. Frowning I sat up and looked around the room for her. Getting off the bed I walked quietly into the living room and saw her on the couch with her head resting on her knees her breathing had gotten shallow. Padding quickly over to her I sat down beside her and put my arm around her shoulders.

"Zoey?" When I didn't get a response I lightly shook her. Her face raised up and stared blankly at the wall behind the TV. "Zoey what's wrong?" her eyes looked as though they had sunken into her head the iris's had turned a deep purple color instead of the lavender or blue gray I had come to love. "Are you hungry?" concern laced through me. She slowly blinked and turned her face to mine, her fangs had doubled in size as her eyes widened at my scent. With a sigh I cupped her face in my hands and pulled her to my neck, slowly sinking into the couch, when our skin met the hair on my arms raised up telling me danger was close by.

"Bite me Zoey, you need to feed." Waiting for her to strike I looked up at the ceiling so I could expose my neck further to give her better access to the vein. A deep rumbling growl bubbled up from her as her body gracefully moved to straddle me. With a strike of a viper her fangs were in my neck and drinking deeply, one hand holding the back of my neck while the other shoved my chin up further to the point of being almost painful. My jaw hardened as she pulled more blood from my system, my head had started getting light as she kept drinking. I felt my body start sagging into the couch more as I released her. When I started blacking out I tried to push her head back from me, but my hand weakly fell back to my side

"Zoey-" my voice was a low whisper as my head lolled backwards into darkness where I blacked out.

Chapter 23

Hurt

—⁓〰⦿⟨⟩⦿〰⁓—

<u>Zoey</u>

I must have fallen asleep on the couch, I was too warm and I kept getting a wonderful taste flooding my mouth. Blinking I realized I was looking at the back of the couch.

"Zoey-" Tara's voice was in my ear, it was almost so low that I couldn't hear it. When I heard a thump I felt my fangs retract from the neck I was sucking on and looked down. I was sitting on top of Tara.

"SHIT!" my eyes widened as her's began rolling into the back of her head, her skin had gone pasty white as her body began seizing. Quickly I began smacking her face lightly trying to wake her up. I heard her heart start to falter as it tried to pump blood weakly through her system. Pulling her off the couch onto the floor I began breathing into her mouth hard. Her chest started lifting as I performed CPR, her heart started fluttering when I breathed into her again. "DAMNIT TARA! BREATH!"

R.J. Young

Running to the bedroom I grabbed the collar I had tossed on the dresser and slid back to her side. Wrapping it around her neck her change immediately forced itself through her system, her body began shaking hard as her limbs grew dark black brown hair. When she whimpered from the pain I moved to her head and held her still in my lap as tears streamed down my face onto her newly forming muzzle. Petting her lightly I heard her heart speed up to an ungodly pace as new blood began coursing through her veins, her loud yelp startled both of us as her body jerked off of my lap as her back started breaking over and over. After a few minutes her body stilled as she panted hard. Her eyes opened slowly with a moan.

"TARA!" rushing over to her I hugged her head into my breasts and cried. "I'm so sorry, I thought I had killed you, I didn't know what else to do I had to do something. Your body wasn't responding to CPR and I didn't want you to die!" I sobbed harder as she licked under my chin and neck weakly. "I love you-" my voice hitched up at the end. She gently pushed away from my chest and looked at me sleepily, she whined gently and wagged her tail slowly. Wiping my eyes tenderly I saw her head tilt towards the kitchen and sniff.

"Are you hungry?" I asked patiently. Her back foot came up and started scratching at the collar causing it to jingle joyfully. Getting up from my kneeling position I kissed between her eyes and wandered to the kitchen. Looking into the fridge I frowned at the shelves, I heard the clicking of claws on the hardwood as Tara came up next to me and sniffed in the cool air of the open door.

"See anything that you want?" I glanced down at her as she snorted. "Alright let's check the freezer." Closing up the fridge I opened the freezer where she gingerly stuck her nose into the cold and used her teeth to pull out a giant frozen prime rib we had bought under Jeremy's instruction.

"Really? You want a steak?" I eyeballed it as she barked at me. "Want it in a doggy bowl or will a plate do?" I teased her as she narrowed her eyes at me. Lifting her leg up again she began scratching at the collar again. "What you want that off so soon?" when she growled I laughed harder. Shaking my head I reached down and began taking it off from around her neck, her change was almost instantaneous as I removed the offending device.

She let out a surprised yelp as she fell to the ground and began twitching and seizing, causing a horrible howling scream to come from her muzzled mouth. Her fur receded back into her skin as her limbs began shrinking and popping back into place shooting her muzzle back into her skull as her face contorted back to her beautiful human features. Turning my back on her to give her a bit of privacy I walked to the stove and pulled out a skillet and turned on the gas burner. I heard her panting from the floor as she was catching her breath from the pain.

Taking the steak out of the air compressed packaging I tossed it onto the heated skillet where it sizzled and let off a strong aroma of thawing meat. I heard her slowly rising from the floor and brace herself onto the counter as her breathing began slowing to a manageable pace. Looking behind myself I saw her slowly sink to the floor, her skin had taken on the color of printer paper as she focused on what looked like not throwing up. Her brow had a light sheen of sweat and her neck had a bruise the size of a fist that had swollen and puckered where I hadn't sealed the bite marks. Walking up to her I squatted down and looked at her.

"Are you okay?" I gently touched the mark on her neck as she jumped and nodded, I felt a surge of shame. I silently vowed to never do that to her again. Her eyes scanned my face as a small flitter of distrust jumped across her features.

"I'm fine" she cleared her throat softly. "I'm just a little sore. It's not everyday I change fully into the-" her lips tightened as she thought of a good word. "Wolf..." Looking away from me she frowned up at the stove. "You're gonna wanna flip that soon. I like it on the medium rare side..." When I turned back to the stove I heard her lean further into the cabinet, peeking back at her again she was looking away from me and staring at the wall in deep thought.

"You... You don't like turning into a wolf?" I asked her tentatively as I flipped the steak over onto its uncooked side, I saw her frown slowly at my question.

"No. It... It scares me every time, I never have control of myself anymore and I am scared that I would hurt you." her head turned to me locking my eyes with hers, we stared at eachother for a heartbeat before she turned away again as she got up onto her feet she spoke. "I just don't want to hurt you one day because I let my control slip just too far and instead of paying attention to what I'm doing I accidentally make a fatal mistake that might cost your life... I just don't want

174

to hurt you..." her head fell as she took a deep breath and turned away from me. I clicked the burner off and rested the steak on a plate I pulled out earlier before walking over and hugging her from behind.

"I know you're scared, I am too. Look what just happened! I didn't even know I was feeding off of someone till I woke up! If anyone should apologize it should be me!" holding her close to me I turned till I was standing in front of her never letting her go. "But we can learn better control together, hell Tara I've been working at this for almost 70 years! And look I still lost control!" Kissing her neck I licked the puncture wounds to help them heal faster. I never realized how much taller she was than me till I really hugged her close, she stood a good two inches above me.

"So are you wanting to wear a suit? Or you wanna go the dress route?" I asked as she laid her head on top of my own.

"For what?" her confusion was evident.

"Well I was thinking perhaps an autumn wedding with the really beautiful navy colors to bring out our eyes. Maybe in a nice park? As long as it's not too cold that is cause my skin will start turning a weird blue color if I get cold." I chuckled lightly as she pulled me closer.

"I think I would like to wear a dress, but I need to get you a ring first before we do anything. Don't want my little woman walking around without her bling." She rubbed my shoulders lightly as her stomach growled.

"Go eat your steak or it's gonna get cold." When I released her I smacked her ass as she walked past causing her to yelp out in surprise. I watched as she grabbed the plate and walked to the couch leaving the fork and knife on the counter behind. I watched as she manhandled the slab of meat and started taking large bites out of it barely tasting before going back for another when her mouth had emptied. "We're gonna have to work on your table manners before the wedding since you're so set on wearing a dress."

She looked up at me with her cheeks puffed out stuffed to the brim with meat. "Iwershengry" she said with her mouth full. After swallowing "Sorry, I haven't eaten and I'm hungry." She shot me a smile and took another huge bite.

Rolling my eyes at her table manners I sat down next to her on the couch and laid my head on her shoulder. Within minutes she had completely destroyed the steak, not even leaving the fat or gristle. With a sigh she sat the plate down on the side table and sank back into the couch with a satisfied expression on her face.

"Thank you for the meal, I was starving." she rubbed her stomach in appreciation.

"You're very welcome, I am glad you enjoyed it." I placed my hand over hers as she rubbed her belly "I never really get to cook good food often because I hardly ever eat anyway. I'm glad food network is gonna come in handy here soon." My hand started trailing down her naked body as she leaned her head back and closed her eyes, I licked a bit of grease off of her collarbone that had dripped onto it causing her to smile my favorite wolfy smile.

Climbing up onto her lap I laid on her chest with a sigh and yawned deep enough to crack my jaw. When she gazed down at me I nuzzled into her neck comfortably as I felt my eyes slowly close.

Tara

When Zoey's eyes closed I smiled down at her and rubbed her back gently, my mind wandered around the thought of seeing her in the forest wearing a wedding dress of her own. When I was sure she had fully fallen asleep I picked her up as carefully as possible and brought her to the bedroom where I laid her on the bed.

Walking to the kitchen I took a spatula off the holding hook under the cabinet and a plastic shopping bag and scraped the collar into it. Holding my prize at arms length I brought it into the bedroom and dumped it onto the dresser. My hand started throbbing being in such close proximity to the large amount of silver, my wolf nails to begin forming making me gasp in pain. Taking a step back from the offending object I walked to the bed and slid under the covers next to Zoey.

When I blinked awake I wasn't even sure when I had passed out, I peeked at the clock and was surprised to find that it was a little past 8pm. Zoey's warm body had curled next to mine tangling our legs together as we rested. Her slow heartbeat comforted me in the warm darkened room, I gently pressed my lips to her forehead and nuzzled her hair breathing in her wonderful fresh rain smell. I felt her stir in my arms as she let out another jaw cracking yawn her body tensed up with a stretch that curled her toes.

"Good evening beautiful." I whispered in her ear.

"What time is it?" she asked sleepily as she yawned again.

"Just after 8pm. I just need my legs back right now cause I'm hungry again." the growl of my stomach punctuated the silence of the room. When she chuckled she lifted her knee up right into my crotch causing me to moan deeply into her neck.

"S-Sorry" she yawned again. "Go get some food and I can finally pleasure you before the day is over. How does that sound?" she smiled up at me like the cheshire cat.

"Go back to sleep you can barely stop yawning just laying here." When she shook her head I thought for a moment. "Well how about this, if you can stay awake in this warm dark room by the time I get back, then you can do whatever you want with me. Within reason of course." I smiled down at her letting the choice be hers.

"You have a deal." her eyes glowed brightly in the darkness. Kissing her tender lips I slowly slipped out of her grasp and walked into the kitchen, mooning her on my way out the door. I began searching the cabinets for something to snack on and came upon precooked bacon and bread. Digging into the fridge I found some mayo and cheese and started constructing a huge sandwich while putting any unused objects away. I took a bite of my creation as I wandered back into the bedroom where Zoey's eyes glowed from the bed. When I smiled at her I heard her chuckle at me and saw the shadows of her arms being held out to come to her. Taking another bite of my sandwich I leaned gracefully on the door frame as she pouted.

"I told you that you could do whatever you wanted to me when I got back, but technically I have not come back. I'm still in the hallway just eating my sandwich" I grinned at her as she crossed her arms. "What are your plans for me my dear?"

"Well… I was thinking that maybe I could test your pain tolerance. Then I thought nah she's a werewolf her tolerance has got to be spot on to change." she grinned widely at me "so then I thought why not tie her up in knots and see what other toys I had hidden away in the drawers and closets of this place." While she was talking I had finished my sandwich and as on the way to the bed to lounge next to her.

"What do you mean tied up in knots?" she had piqued my curiosity.

"Wait right here and I will show by example." When she wandered over to the closet I heard her digging somewhere deep in the back before emerging with what seemed to be a metal bar with leather handcuffs on it. The building of passion flew through me as she placed it on the bed next to me. A slow easy smile spread across my face as she leaned into me for a kiss.

"Lay down beautiful." she whispered in my ear. As I complied her cool touch made me jump as she grabbed my ankles. Looking at her she fastened the leather cuff to one leg and began twisting the bar to release it from the threading, extending it out to about four feet. When she grabbed my free ankle and strapped me in my legs were bound tightly as though I were a dangerous animal. When she walked to my hands I presented them for her to bind them into the middle of the bed with the scarf that was draped through the little silver O hook. When my hands were fully tied up she walked to the end of the bed and smiled down at her handiwork. I watched as she walked gracefully danced over to the closet and pulled out a black hat box with a red silk bow on top, as she removed the lid I saw an assortment of leather objects. One in particular caught my eye, when she pulled it out my eyes widened slightly. It was a long curved object that looked like a dildo but only had a little bend at the tip.

"This is called a G-spot stimulator, I just need one crucial part of this one first before we get started so just sit tight." she shot me a grin as she walked out of room leaving me tied up. Tugging on the bonds lightly I chuckled when I had just a little give to the material. I heard her banging around in the kitchen in what sounded like the freezer, when the door closed I heard her footsteps pad through the hall till she was once again in the doorway. The G-spot stimulator in one hand and the metal had frosted over lightly while the other hand held a plastic cup. As she walked to her side of the bed she placed the cup on the table, it had been filled to the brim with ice. Zoey walked between my legs again and licked her lips slowly as her eyes slowly changed to a light lavender color.

"Brace yourself my love. This will be intense." as he climbed up between my legs I felt her sit on top of the bar holding my feet flat onto the bed while bending my knees. Slowly she licked the new toy from base to tip till it was covered in her saliva and dissipating the frost. When she leaned down I felt a huge chill at my opening causing me to gasp loudly. The cold spread up through my legs till I was shivering with anticipation and pleasure.

As she slowly began inserting the toy into me the cold chill began to flow up my body causing my nipples to harden. My moan echoed through the room as she pushed it fully into my sex as my toes curled with excitement. I felt her get up from her spot leaving the toy inside me. Looking at her I saw as she reached for an ice cube from her little cup and pop it into her mouth. When she sat on the bar again she leaned into me and began pulling and pushing at the toy lightly causing me to arch up in surprise. Her mouth came down to my nipple causing me to hiss as the ice cube touched the bare skin. When her tongue twirled it around my areola I felt my toes spread and curl as I tugged at my bonds while her hand kept gently playing with the toy between my legs.

As she sped up her pace I felt my eyes roll into the back of my head as I gasped in shock when her thumb began to work my clitoris. My orgasm wasn't far behind as she worked and played between my breasts and legs I felt it shatter me from behind. My inner walls contracted as it hit me like a brick wall causing my hips to thras on the bed till my breathing caught in my throat. When my chest rattled I felt myself slip into darkness and I slipped into a satisfied sleep.

Zoey

As I gazed down at Tara I felt a sense of wonder staring at her naked form. Gently I unbuckled her legs from the bar and untied her hands from the scarf, when her arms gently slipped down to the bed I smiled down at her. My eyes trailed down her body with reverence till I looked between her legs where the toy was still deep within her. Climbing on top to where I was sitting on her hips I gently began tugging lightly on the cool metal trying to remove it. Her opening throbbed at my pulls causing her to arch lightly as a moan escaped from her lips.

Peeking behind myself I saw her eyes flutter open for a moment before a yawn opened her mouth wide, when she squinted at me her eyes spiraled out into the lovely gold color. A deep rumbling came from her parted lips as her hands traced up my thighs in a loving gesture before resting on my hip bones, her nostrils flared slightly as she took in my scent. Her ascending growl was almost a question as she gently began pulling my hips towards her face. I noticed as she tugged me lightly that her eyes had taken on an animalistic reflective shine to them.

When my ass had come within a few inches of her mouth I felt her tongue snake into me causing my body to involuntarily arch up with a gasp, her nails began digging into the meaty part of my thighs as she held me in place. As her tongue lapped at my sex an appreciative growly bubbled out through her lips and zipped through me at breakneck speed causing me to squirm into her mouth and pushing her face further into myself. As her tongue moved down further till it had rested onto my clit it began dancing wildly till I was bucking and thrashing like a bull rider.

Before I knew what was happening my orgasim rammed me in the back like a bulldozer causing me to fall forward in a sweaty panting pile of pleasure. I felt her hands snake their way around my torso as she dragged me upwards till she was spooning against me and holding my arms in place, her right leg kicked over my hip and pulling me tight against her so I wouldn't be able to move even if I had wanted to. I felt my eyes droop in satisfaction as her heated breath tickled the back of my neck lulling me into a slow and contented dreamless sleep.

Chapter 24

Gone

―――‿∿‿⦾⋐⦿⋑⦾‿∿‿―――

Tara

I woke up very warm but sore. Slowly opening my eyes I noticed Zoey's deep chocolate colored hair was skewing my vision, the perfume of her skin was all around me filling my nose. A slow easy smile spread across my face as I gently began caressing down her arm till my hand rested on her hip. When she stirred from her slumber I heard her take in a long yawn as she turned to face me, her smile matched mine in the dim glow of the bedroom. When my hand began moving inward towards her private area I felt her body tense up slightly at my touch.

"Everything okay beautiful?" I could hear the worry in my voice as she slowly relaxed against my touch. When I used a feather light touch on the hair between her legs her thighs began spreading themselves open till I could fit my hand between them to gently rub her folds.

"Everything is-" Her mouth dropped into an O shape. "Ah!

My god!" when my hand teased its way inside her she arched slowly up like a cat. Her breathing became shallow as I gently petted inside her walls till I had her panting, my own wetness began soaking my leg in need as I watched her squirm. When her hand came between my legs I felt a minor resistance in my own walls till her fingers caressed me softly.

As we gently masturbated each other our breathing began to sync up as our fingers moved at a faster pace, both hands becoming slick with greed and lust. As we climaxed we held our bodies close together as our hips swayed on the others hand that was buried deep within the other. When we finished we collapsed onto the bed both breathing heavily, looking into her eyes I leaned in close and kissed her sweetly.

"Do you know of any good bars in the area? Like the kind that you can spend the whole night dancing into exhaustion?" My curiosity perked up as she thought for a moment.

"I believe there is one, it's more of a club than anything. But it is where our kind go to mingle and meet each other." When I frowned she continued with her explanation. "It's better for our kind to meet others like us. When we get a normal person in our beds sometimes it doesn't end very well, especially if we get them pregnant."

"Why is that? Do the babies not survive or something?" I felt my frown deepen as my mind wandered a bit.

"Well sometimes yes that can happen, it's more about the one carrying them. The mother of the child will have intense cravings, not normal cravings like pickles and ice cream but weird cravings. Think of it this way, a male vampire gets a human pregnant right? Well that mother as the pregnancy progresses she is going to have cravings for blood. It can be very detrimental to the health and well being of the human and the infant. With werewolves I know the mothers tend to crave rare meats." With a smile she kissed my forehead that had wrinkled up with my thoughts.

"So... if we choose to have a child, will we use a male vampire? So it would have both vampire and werewolf in it?" I felt Zoey tense up next to me. "What? Did I say something wrong?" I slowly pulled away from her to see her biting on her lip in worry.

"No, it's nothing wrong. It's just that when you mix species sometimes the offsprings don't come out normal, and sometimes they don't survive... I mean we can try that's not a problem but I want you to know it could be a bad situation. Are you prepared for that?"

Thinking about what she told me I felt my stomach start doing flips at the possibility of having a child with Zoey. Looking into her worried face I slowly smiled. "I might not be ready for losing a child. I don't think anyone is ever truly ready... but I do want to try." I saw her lips purse together as she slowly nodded her head.

"How about this then, We go see some of my friends and talk over the possibility of them giving us a... donation Of sorts." it wasn't a question but mostly a suggestion her forehead creased just a little bit showing lines of worry and thought. "The thing is we have maybe 3-4 other vampires who would maybe want to do this for us so we have limited chances to use them."

I grabbed her by her shoulders and pulled her into my chest holding her into a hug. "Let's make some appointments with them then."

Looking over her head I saw Atlas had wandered through the open doorway and had laid down onto the beds rejected comforter, his tail was wagging a mile a minute. Zoey followed my stare and noticed Atlas and grinned as his tongue lolled out of his mouth.

"He hasn't been outside for a little bit, maybe we should take him on a walk?" She looked over at me. I felt my eyes swirl with color at the mention of going outside. Atlas lept up from the blanket and walked briskly out the room where I heard him scratching lightly at the door.

"That sounds like a good idea. We should probably get dressed first and take him to the park. Maybe teach him how to catch a frisbee?"

"Are you in control right now?" her brow wrinkled again in worry.

"Yup fit as a fiddle, just excited is all." I slowly got up and wandered to the closet to find something to wear. "Do you think tonight we could go to the club you were talking about earlier? Maybe grab Jeremy and Tom and just have a night?"

"That would be fun I'll text them to let them know." I felt her arms wrap around me as she peeked over my shoulder into the closet. Her hand shot out and grabbed a pale blue button up with dark skinny jeans. Looking at the other clothes I grabbed an army green three quarter sleeved shirt and boot-cut pants. As I turned out from the closet Zoey wandered out of the bathroom fully dressed and grabbed Atlas's leash from the small hook by the door she had installed a few days ago.

"I'm gonna take him out while you get ready just meet me downstairs." Blowing a kiss at me she walked out the door with Atlas in tow.

Slipping my shirt over my head I could feel the excitement building in my stomach. I had everything I could ever want; a woman who loves me, a well behaved dog, and a sense of home. Nothing could have been more perfect.

Once I was presentable I walked to the door and slipped on my shoes, grabbing my keys from the little side table I stuffed them into my pocket. Opening the door I saw a tall man standing in front of me and a fist coming right at my face.

The impact sent me flying back over our couch and sliding me into the wall knocking the breath out of me. Rolling over with a groan I was seeing stars from my head throbbing, when I looked down my nose had started gushing blood all over my green top. I felt a pair of strong arms hoist me up as the brute flung me into our tv stand. Crashing into the tv my ears began ringing with pain as I felt my shoulder blade shatter into a million pieces.

Looking upwards at the asshole I saw his boot come down onto my face before I didn't see anything anymore.

Chapter 25

Pain

---~~~⌇⌇⌇⌇~~~---

Zoey

My head was throbbing like a train chugging through a tunnel. It felt like the time I had fallen out of my grandmother's tree in her backyard trying to climb to the top. I tried rotating my shoulders a little bit to see if anything was broken and found that I couldn't move at all. Slowly opening my eyes my vision swam as the world spun out of control. Closed was better my ears picked up little noises throughout the room I heard one person sobbing softly and hiccuping between breaths.

"Tom?" My voice was hoarse and my mouth was dry.

"Zoey!" he exclaimed in a deep whisper "oh thank the gods you're okay! They have Tara! They have Tara and Jeremy, there was so much blood. I don't know what's happening are you are you hurting?" his voice wavered between sobs.

"I can't open my eyes and my head hurts but I think I'm okay... how bad is this?" My voice cracked with worry.

"It's really bad. I watched them bring Tara through right after they put you in there. She didn't look so good." his breath hitched again pathetically.

Taking a deep breath I slowly opened my eyes through the pain. The blinding fluorescent lights stabbed through my corneas till my stomach started turning, breathing through the pain I slowly raised my head to look around. Tom had been tied up with thick ropes as snot and blood dripped from his nose with tears streaking his cheeks that had turned black and blue from heavy bruises covering his normally tanned skin. I slowly turned onto my back till I was looking up at the blank ceiling and successfully crushing my hands under me. Peeking down at myself I saw I had been roped also.

Looking over at Tom I felt a surge of anger dart through me at how we had been treated. My nostrils flared out as the perfume of blood saturated the little room, I couldn't help myself as my fangs began elongating till they were deadly points. My head began pounding further as my energy began to plummet. With a surge I forced myself to sit up till I was able to cross my legs over themselves.

"T-Tom I may have an idea on how to get us out of here. You're gonna have to trust me though ok?" I saw a flash of fear pass over his face before his mouth hardened into a thin line of determination. "I need a donation from you if we want to get out of here. Right now I don't have the strength but all I need is maybe a cup of blood…"

Tom lifted his head up till he was staring at the ceiling in acceptance. As he closed his eyes I saw his Adam's apple bob in fear a few times. "Zoey, I've never thought I'd say this but... bite me girl. Just make it fast."

Scooting myself till I was seated right next to him I stared at the plump vein in his neck in hunger. Without any warning I struck out and latched onto his neck like a leech. His blood immediately flooded my mouth in a spicy and tantalizing flavor that surged to my core. I felt my body shiver slightly as I drank deeply into his vein. The muscles in my arms began to throb with power. Taking my fangs from his neck I licked the puncture wounds gently to get the healing process running. Scooting away from Tom I saw him slowly lower his head back down as he leaned into the wall once again.

"Now what?" he said in a very raspy voice. Before he could continue I stretched my arms out to the side till the ropes creaked and stretched to the point of snapping behind my back. Breathing heavily I slumped over onto myself trying to hold my body from falling fully.

"Now it's your turn..." scooting over to Tom again I used my fingernails that had grown sharp and pointed to slice Tom's bindings from him. Once cut loose he grasped his wrists and began rubbing them vigorously to get the blood flowing to them again.

I began looking around the room in a panic. There was just a simple door no windows with a regular door handle on it.

It can't be that simple can it?

Slowly getting up I twisted the knob till I heard the handle's tumblers bust apart. Looking over at Tom he got up and limped over to me till he was by my side, pulling the door open we heard a horrible shriek as though someone was being murdered.

With one last look at Tom we raced out the door to follow the sound.

Tara

My eyes felt heavy and everything hurt all over. I slowly opened my heavily bruised lids to see Jeremy laying in a pool of blood. His chest was rising and falling gently so he was at least alive, I gently turned my head and took in my surroundings till they rested upon two figures standing in front of the door. One was a plump woman with long hair wearing a skirt an expression of anger and annoyance. The man standing at her side was stall and had graying hair with a long hooked nose and a face filled with malice.

Andy and Stephanie LaRenge the people responsible for all of the abuse both mentally and physically. The people who at the drop of the hat would turn a fun "family" outing into an all out war. Just seeing Andy grinning like the asshole he is sent chills down my spine.

"Tara, we are so glad you could join us. We hope this mutt hasn't been troubling you and filling your head with impure thoughts." My mother spoke softly at me. "perhaps we should teach our "dear" nephew what happens in a pack when you anger an alpha. What do you think Andy?" My mother's eyes flashed a poison green color as she looked at her husband.

Without a word Andy reached in his back pocket and pulled out a long hunting knife and sauntered over to Jeremy.

"NO! LEAVE HIM ALONE!" my voice rang out loudly I scrambled over to my fallen cousin and laid over his prone form. My son of a bitch father grabbed my arm and yanked me off of him till I helped with pain. I could feel the panic building in my chest, my heart began racing till I felt a scream bubble though my lips. My parents looked over at me in shock as I released my wolf out and sprouted fur and a muzzle. My father turned to me with the knife and I saw the blade shine in the light a horrible silver color. My lips peeled back till all of my teeth were showing.

Lunging at him I felt the cold metal knick my ear as I bit down on his wrist in a bone crushing way till the knife dropped from his grip, his other hand was smashing into the side of my face trying to pry my mouth free.

My teeth sank deeper till he began screaming loudly, his blood filled my mouth and flooded down my throat like gas to a flame. I felt my vision go red as I began ripping and shredding at his chest with anything my paws and legs could hit, he tumbled backwards over Jeremy as I kept biting harder. Seeing my opportunity I lunged for his throat and in one fluid motion ripped his esophagus out of his neck, splattering blood everywhere. His body jerked once then twice as I watched the life leave his eyes.

Looking over my shoulder I saw an open door and no sign of my mother anywhere. Breathing heavily I laid down next to Jeremy just as Zoey and Tom ran in. My vision blanked out and I felt myself falling into the pit of darkness.

Chapter 26

Relief

───ⁿⁿ~ᕬᘏᕬᘏᕬ~ⁿⁿ───

Tara

It's been three months since the incident with my parents and we haven't heard anything from my mother. Zoey tried to follow the scent of her blood but to no avail. Jeremy had been knocked unconscious and has recovered nicely since then. Atlas had found his way back to our apartment and got into a few things while we had been gone but nothing too major.

Today is Zoey and mines anniversary and I have the best gift in the whole world. I took a pregnancy test this morning and it came back positive.

This will be the best day ever...

The End